"Dennis Johnson ably
Jesus understood that
Journeys with Jesus helps us to see the proper ways in which
the Old Testament is Christ-centered, and to read the Old
Testament Christianly. I commend this book to readers, who
will benefit from following Jesus' approach to interpreting
the Old Testament. In doing so, they will discover the many
glorious ways in which the Old Testament points to Jesus as
its goal."

> —**G. K. Beale**, J. Gresham Machen Chair of New Testament
> and Professor of New Testament and Biblical Theology,
> Westminster Theological Seminary

"I rejoice to read Dennis Johnson's *Journeys with Jesus: Exploring
How the Whole Bible Leads Us to Christ.* Johnson's long-term
study of how the message of our Savior pervades all of Scripture
combines with his preaching expertise to set our hearts on fire
for the glory of the gospel in all of life. The added expertise of
longtime mission educator Richard Ramsay makes this book a
great resource that will enable all cultures to learn, and delight
in, the grace that threads through the Bible from beginning
to end."

> —**Bryan Chapell**, Pastor, Grace Presbyterian Church, Peo-
> ria, Illinois; President Emeritus, Covenant Theological
> Seminary

"Dennis Johnson leads us by the hand along the desert road
where the Ethiopian eunuch met Philip in the book of Acts, as
he sought help in understanding the Bible's message. Like Philip,
Dr. Johnson focuses our gaze on the crucified, risen, and glorified Messiah, Jesus, as the central message of the Scriptures. In
the process, he teaches us how to trace these biblical connections

with greater skill, both for our own personal benefit and so that we can better teach others."

— **Iain M. Duguid**, Professor of Old Testament, Westminster Theological Seminary

"Others have written on how the Old Testament leads to Christ. What makes *Journeys with Jesus* stand out is that it is written by a *New Testament* scholar. Some treatments present Christ as merely the solution to an Old Testament puzzle. But once the puzzle is solved, we learn little about the Savior *himself*. Strong on hermeneutical techniques, they are weak on Christ. By contrast, Dennis Johnson expounds the organic character of redemptive history with a deep appreciation for New Testament Christology. This is an essential combination and makes *Journeys with Jesus* an outstandingly helpful book."

— **Sinclair B. Ferguson**, Chancellor's Professor of Systematic Theology, Reformed Theological Seminary

"Redemptive-historical hermeneutics has been a major topic among Reformed scholars. What it means is simply that every part of the Bible teaches Christ, and that the most important thing about every passage is what it teaches us about him. Many pastors interpret biblical texts this way in their sermons, but they don't always explain to the congregation what they are doing. Dennis Johnson's *Journeys with Jesus* explains the concept well. Johnson shows us how we can read the Bible ourselves in a Christ-centered way, and how this approach enriches our understanding of the Word of God."

— **John M. Frame**, Professor of Systematic Theology and Philosophy Emeritus, Reformed Theological Seminary, Orlando

"Hearts burned on the road to Emmaus as Christ explained the Scriptures. The same fire burns in the New Testament, written by those whose minds Jesus opened. Dennis Johnson carries the fire, and he wants you to feel it, too. Join him on the road."

—**James M. Hamilton**, Professor of Biblical Theology, The Southern Baptist Theological Seminary

"Dennis Johnson taught me how to find Christ in all the Scriptures when I was his student. After all these years, now as a colleague, I still jump at the chance to hear his rich explorations of the greatest story ever told. Read this book and you'll never read *the* Book the same way again."

—**Michael S. Horton**, J. Gresham Machen Professor of Systematic Theology and Apologetics, Westminster Seminary California

"The invitation given by Dennis Johnson to journey through the whole Bible with Jesus is challenging and exciting. Anything written by Dr. Johnson is bound to be theologically sound and intellectually stimulating. This book is more than that. It comes from the heart of a man who has walked with Jesus in his personal life as well as in his study of the Scriptures. Dennis Johnson knows Jesus and knows how to help others to know him."

—**Rosemary Jensen**, Founder and President, Rafiki Foundation

"I know of no better guide than Dennis Johnson in helping sojourners see the beauty of Jesus in all the Scriptures. With a wonderful balance of clear explanation and compelling inspiration, this book will open up the minds and hearts of those in the pulpit and in the pew. Every Christian who longs for more wisdom and strength for their pilgrim journey needs this book to help them see the beauty and wonder found in the person and work of Jesus."

    —**Julius J. Kim**, Dean of Students & Professor of Practical Theology, Westminster Seminary California

"Like every other Christian, I long to walk more closely and constantly with Jesus. This book helped me to refine my walk by showing me more of Jesus throughout the Bible. It was an easy and delightful read, and it's sure to ignite many hearts."

    —**David Murray**, Professor of Old Testament, Puritan Reformed Theological Seminary; Pastor, Grand Rapids Free Reformed Church

JOURNEYS
WITH JESUS

JOURNEYS WITH JESUS

EVERY PATH IN THE BIBLE LEADS US TO CHRIST

An Abridged Edition of *Walking with Jesus through His Word: Discovering Christ in All the Scriptures*

DENNIS E. JOHNSON

Abridged by Richard B. Ramsay

P&R PUBLISHING

P.O. BOX 817 • PHILLIPSBURG • NEW JERSEY 08865-0817

This is an abridged edition of *Walking with Jesus through His Word: Discovering Christ in All the Scriptures* © 2015 by Dennis E. Johnson (P&R Publishing).

Unless otherwise indicated, all Scripture quotations are from the ESV® Bible (The Holy Bible, English Standard Version®), copyright © 2001 by Crossway, a publishing ministry of Good News Publishers. Used by permission. All rights reserved.

Scripture quotations marked (NASB) are taken from the New American Standard Bible®, copyright © 1960, 1962, 1963, 1968, 1971, 1972, 1973, 1975, 1977, 1995 by The Lockman Foundation Used by permission.

Italics within Scripture quotations indicate emphasis added.

ISBN: 978-1-62995-538-4 (pbk)
ISBN: 978-1-62995-539-1 (ePub)
ISBN: 978-1-62995-540-7 (Mobi)

Printed in the United States of America

Library of Congress Cataloging-in-Publication Data

Names: Johnson, Dennis E. (Dennis Edward), author.
Title: Journeys with Jesus : every path in the Bible leads us to Christ / Dennis E. Johnson.
Other titles: Walking with Jesus through his word
Description: Abridged [edition] / by Richard P. Ramsay. | Phillipsburg : P&R Publishing, 2018. | Abridged ed. of: Walking with Jesus through his word : discovering Christ in all the scriptures. 2015. | Includes index.
Identifiers: LCCN 2018010787| ISBN 9781629955384 (pbk.) | ISBN 9781629955391
(epub) | ISBN 9781629955407 (mobi)
Subjects: LCSH: Bible. Old Testament--Introductions. | Jesus Christ.
Classification: LCC BS1140.3 .J632 2018 | DDC 220.6--dc23
LC record available at https://lccn.loc.gov/2018010787

To Our Children:
Eric and Susanne
Christina and Julien
Peter and Mandi
Laurie and Daniel

And Their Children:
Jonathan, Simeon, Andrew, Gabriel,
Kellen, Zane, Logan,
Maya, Naomi, Peyton, Sophia,
Carter, Finnan, Keziah,
Iain, Claire

He commanded our fathers
to teach to their children,
that the next generation might know them,
the children yet unborn,
and arise and tell them to their children,
so that they should set their hope in God
and not forget the works of God,
but keep his commandments.
(Psalm 78:5–7)

CONTENTS

FOREWORD

I WAS TAKING questions in a Q&A session at a large church when a woman asked, "How can I find things in the Bible I want to read about—like how to deal with anger or fear?" I heard in her question a profound but very common misunderstanding of what the Bible is and how to approach it. She saw the Bible as a source of good advice about how to manage the difficulties of life, and she wanted to mine it for answers to her particular questions and needs. In other words, she wanted to set the agenda for what she wanted to know from God based on what she assumed she needed most to hear from God.

But that's not what the Bible is for or how it works. While there is comfort to be found from the Bible, what we read in it is often more troubling than comforting. While there is wisdom to be found in the Bible, we also witness incredible foolishness in the people we read about in its pages. And while there are certainly answers to very real and important questions in the Bible, the more we read it, we discover that it answers questions that we didn't even know enough to ask. It is telling us what we most need to know.

Rather than accommodating our desire for the Bible to address what we think is most important, the Bible invites us to allow it to show us what is most important. And what is most important—from start to finish—is Christ. More relevant than what you are supposed to do is what *he* has done. More essential to who you should be is who *he* is.

But many of us simply didn't grow up learning how to read and understand the Bible this way. We are in need of retraining, in some cases a complete reorientation to how to read and understand the Bible with Christ at the center. That's exactly what Dennis Johnson provides to us in this book. He hands us tools to use on the text to help us unearth the treasure of seeing Christ. He gives us new lenses to see the picture being painted of our Redeemer, Savior, Prophet, Priest, and King in all of the Bible's historical narrative, law, poetry, discourse, and apocalypse. He helps us to hear the drumbeat of the first coming of Christ and kindles in our hearts a longing for him to come again. Best of all, he invites us on a journey with Jesus that will lead us into richer relationship and greater worship.

Nancy Guthrie
Bible teacher, author, and
host of the *Help Me Teach the Bible* podcast

ACKNOWLEDGMENTS

NONE OF US learns to read the Bible alone. The apostles needed Jesus to help them see in the Scriptures the things concerning himself (Luke 24). Early Christians needed the apostles' teaching (Acts 2:42). In every generation the church needs teachers and pastors, given by our risen Lord (Eph. 4:11). So whatever you find useful here, as you study God's Word, you can rest assured that I have learned it from others. I have spared you a flood of footnotes to make *Journeys with Jesus* more readable. (If you thrive on delving into documentation and checking sources, feel free to start with my *Him We Proclaim* and the other resources listed in "For Further Reading" at the end of this book.)

I am glad to acknowledge those through whom I have come to see how the tapestry of Scripture and the history of redemption find their focus and coherence in the Lord Jesus Christ. Some have taught me in person, through formal instruction and informal conversation: Derke P. Bergsma, Edmund P. Clowney, Raymond B. Dillard, Iain M. Duguid, Bryan D. Estelle, John M. Frame, Mark D. Futato, Richard B. Gaffin Jr., Robert H. Gundry, Michael S. Horton, Vern S. Poythress, and O. Palmer Robertson. Others have taught me through their publications: G. K. Beale, Bryan Chapell, Sinclair Ferguson, R. T. France, Graeme Goldsworthy, Leonhard Goppelt, Sidney Greidanus, Meredith G. Kline, Tremper Longman III, Geerhardus Vos, and Christopher J. H. Wright. From many of these I have learned both in person and in print.

My colleagues on the faculty of Westminster Seminary California were kind enough to read and discuss parts of *Walking with Jesus through His Word*, the longer book that is abridged here. Their comments helped to improve clarity, and for those observations I am thankful. I'm even more grateful for our shared commitment across our various disciplines—biblical studies, theology, homiletics—to point students to Christ as the center of God's Word.

My hope for *Walking with Jesus through His Word* was that it would serve leaders of the global church. Yet when it was published, wise counselors observed that in translation it would likely be too long to attract many readers. One of those who offered this counsel, Richard Ramsay, did more than recommend abridgment: he did the painful work of abridging (and rearranging—and illustrating) *Walking with Jesus* by over 50 percent, for the sake of producing an accessible Spanish translation of reasonable length, which he and his wife, Angelica, are doing. More than that, Rich offered the draft of the English abridgment to me and P&R for readers of English. Thus, you now hold *Journeys with Jesus*. Rich and I were seminary classmates in the early 1970s, and we are ministers in the Presbyterian Church in America. He serves the Spanish-speaking church with the PCA's Mission to the World, first in Chile for twenty-one years and now with Third Millennium Ministries. I am glad to be working with him (across the miles) after all these years, and I am grateful for the Ramsays' efforts to make this material accessible to both Spanish and English readers. Rich also provided the helpful illustration of the biblical "terrain" that leads to Christ, which you will repeatedly see in the following chapters.

As they always do, the editorial staff of P&R Publishing has improved this book in the process of preparing it for publication. John J. Hughes has not only managed the editorial process adroitly, but also recommended additions to the work that will make it more useful to readers. Copyeditor Karen Magnuson's sharp eyes and mind caught and corrected errors; and she raised questions that diagnosed obscurity and suggested remedies, resulting in greater clarity, for which readers will be grateful.

I thank God that for decades my family and I have been well fed spiritually, week by week, by hearing Christ preached from all the Scriptures at New Life Presbyterian Church in Escondido, California. Our pastor, Ted Hamilton, has led us in journeys with Jesus through the vast landscape of Scripture and shown us the difference it makes in life's everyday joys and struggles.

I am especially grateful for Jane, my beloved "helper who fits" me just right (Gen. 2:18) for over four decades. For this project, as for every previous one, she has been my first sharp-eyed reader, my insightful editor, and my constant encourager.

Finally, human words—even the best of them—fail to express the thanks that I want to offer to the triune God, who revealed himself to us and reconciled us to himself through the incarnation of the Son, Jesus the Christ, and through his redemptive achievement on our behalf. My prayer is that you will be drawn to praise him with me as we journey with Jesus through the Bible, from Genesis through Revelation.

1

BEGINNING THE JOURNEY

The Walk through the Bible That Sets Hearts Afire

THE TITLE OF this book implies an audacious claim: all sixty-six books in the Bible, which were written by many people over many centuries, are united by one central theme, a single plotline, and a unique Hero, Jesus the Messiah. Of course, two-thirds of these Scriptures were written long before Jesus was born in Bethlehem, and do not mention him by name. Moreover, these documents come in different forms: historical narratives, law codes, wisdom aphorisms, theological discourses, poems, letters, symbolic visions, and more. Nevertheless, I want to persuade you that Jesus is the central figure in the Bible because he is central to the outworking of God's plan for all of history. Moreover, this book proposes a way of reading Scripture that is rooted in Scripture itself and that will equip you to appreciate how the whole Bible reveals Christ and his mission of rescue and renovation.

We will analyze many details of biblical interpretation,

using the figure of a landscape with rivers, a lake, and mountains. We want to develop an explorer's eye to spot directional clues, so that we won't "get lost in the forest," but always keep the big picture in mind as we move toward our destination.

In this introductory chapter, we will answer the following questions:

- What does it mean to journey with Jesus through the Bible?
- Does *all of the Bible* really talk about Jesus?
- Why is it important to learn to journey with Jesus through the Bible?

All Roads Lead to London

In a sermon on 1 Peter 2:7, entitled "Christ Precious to Believers," the great nineteenth-century preacher Charles Spurgeon attributed this story to a Welsh preacher: A young preacher had preached in the presence of a respected older pastor. Afterward, he asked what the old minister thought of his sermon. The old preacher said that it was "a very poor sermon indeed."

The young man had worked a long time on the sermon and was shocked to be told that it was so poor. He asked where the problem lay: Did he not explain the text well? Yes, said the seasoned pastor, his explanation was "very good indeed." Weren't his metaphors appropriate and his arguments conclusive? They, too, were "very good as far as that goes," but still it was "a very poor sermon." Finally, the young man asked what the defect was that made his sermon so poor, and the answer came back: "*There was no Christ in it.*"

Now the young man began to defend himself, objecting, "Well, Christ was not in the text; we are not to be preaching

Christ always, we must preach what is in the text." In response, the older pastor drew this analogy: "Don't you know, young man, that from every town, and every village, and every little hamlet in England, wherever it may be, there is a road to London?"

"Yes," said the young man.

"Ah!" said the old divine, "and so from every text in Scripture, there is a road to the metropolis of the Scriptures, that is Christ. And my dear brother, your business is when you get to a text, to say, 'Now what is the road to Christ?' and then preach a sermon, running along the road towards the great metropolis—Christ. And," said he, "I have never yet found a text that had not got a road to Christ in it, and if I ever do find one that has not a road to Christ in it, I will make one; I will go over hedge and ditch but I would get at my Master, for the sermon cannot do any good unless there be a savour of Christ in it."[1]

Often when Spurgeon's story is retold, attention is drawn to the statement about going "over hedge and ditch" to reach Christ, whatever it takes to get there. Some who read Spurgeon's sermons may even suspect that Spurgeon himself does his share of climbing hedges and fording ditches, overlooking a passage's original context, in order to connect it, somehow or other, to the person and redeeming work of Jesus. When we sense that some interpreter's clever ingenuity has "blazed the trail" from an Old Testament passage to Christ, it makes us suspicious of the suggestion that routes really exist that lead to Christ from passages written centuries before his birth.

1. Charles H. Spurgeon, "Christ Precious to Believers" (March 13, 1859), no. 242, in *The New Park Street Pulpit*, vol. 5 (1860; repr., Grand Rapids: Zondervan, 1964), 140; also available at http://www.romans45.org/spurgeon/sermons/0242.htm.

Now, let me say two things in defense of Spurgeon's little parable. First, the old minister was correct to say that unless our engagement with Scripture enables us to taste the "savour"—the aroma—of the Savior, it cannot do us any real spiritual good. Since God speaks truth and defines goodness in the Bible, many people use it merely as a manual of doctrine or a guidebook for living. But our minds will remain blind to God's truth, our hearts cold to his love, and our wills resistant to his commands, unless his Holy Spirit intervenes to transform us. That transformation happens only when we encounter the astonishing good news about the undeserved mercy that God has shown toward us in his Son. So the seasoned pastor's passion to bring his hearers to Jesus at all costs is exactly right.

Second, notice the real point of the old preacher's analogy between the Bible and the English road system. Every hamlet in England, no matter how small or remote, is linked, somehow or other, to London, the capital of the kingdom. If a bewildered tourist asks directions to the great metropolis, no honest villager would ever say, "Sorry, you cannot get there from here." So also the Bible tells one coherent story that, despite all its diversity in details, is focused on one majestic Hero and directed toward the climax of one cosmic conflict. In a lifetime of ministry, the old pastor had never found a biblical text that had no connection to Jesus. We should therefore approach every text in the Bible expecting that God has actually laid out a path, a lane, an avenue, or a superhighway by which we can travel from that passage, with its unique message in its distinctive location in the history of redemption and revelation, to its fulfillment in Christ. Our challenge, then, is not to hack our way through dense forest, but to discern the routes that the Bible's Designer has already embedded in its landscape.

In other words, we need the divine Author of the Bible to

teach us how to read the Bible. The means by which he does this is the Bible itself, since it is in the pages of Scripture that God speaks infallibly, inerrantly, and most clearly. As wise pastors and theologians stated several centuries ago, "The infallible rule of interpretation of Scripture is the Scripture itself: and therefore, when there is a question about the true and full sense of any Scripture (which is not manifold, but one), it must be searched and known by other places that speak more clearly" (Westminster Confession of Faith [WCF] 1.9).

On the Road to Emmaus

In this first chapter, we join a group of three travelers as they walk together the seven-mile (11 km) journey from ancient Jerusalem to a small town called Emmaus. They are Cleopas and his colleague—two heartbroken disciples—and a stranger.

It was the same day that Jesus had risen, the third day after his brutal, bloody execution by crucifixion. Some women came to the tomb in which his body had been placed in haste two days earlier. In their love and grief they planned to prepare his body for burial more adequately than they could before the Sabbath began. At the tomb, now empty, they saw angels, who announced that Jesus was risen, as he had foretold. Immediately the women carried the word to the apostles and others (Luke 24:1–12).

Cleopas and his companion had heard the women's report, but they didn't believe it. They left for Emmaus, and were discussing the discouraging events of the past week. Jesus had received a royal welcome as he entered David's city just a week earlier, but had been repudiated by his people and their leaders and executed by the Roman authorities.

A stranger joined them on the road—a stranger to them, not to us, for our narrator identifies him as Jesus but comments that "their eyes were kept from recognizing him" (Luke 24:16). When he asked what they had been discussing, they poured out their disillusionment and confusion. Then the stranger, who seemed so ignorant of recent events, replied:

> O foolish ones, and slow of heart to believe all that the prophets have spoken! Was it not necessary that the Christ should suffer these things and enter into his glory? (vv. 25–26)

We might expect that such a blunt rebuke from a stranger would halt the conversation, but the mysterious stranger kept right on talking:

> And beginning with Moses and all the Prophets, he interpreted to them in all the Scriptures the things concerning himself. (v. 27)

Jesus traced their dismay to unbelief, a foolish and sluggish reluctance to trust what God had spoken through Israel's ancient prophets. The ancient Scriptures given through Moses and the Prophets—our Old Testament—showed that God had planned all along for the Messiah to suffer a humiliating and violent death, but then to "enter into his glory"—a reversal that is explained in detail in Luke's account of a second Bible study later that evening.

The unrecognized traveler's explanation of Scripture set their hearts afire with hope and joy; so when they reached Emmaus, Cleopas and his companion prevailed on him to join them for supper. As he took the role of the dinner host, breaking the bread (as he had done a few evenings before, instituting the Lord's Supper), suddenly they recognized Jesus. Then he vanished.

In Jerusalem

They immediately returned to Jerusalem, where they found that the risen Lord Jesus had appeared to Simon Peter, as he had to them. Then, in the midst of this larger group of disciples, Jesus appeared again, demonstrated the physical reality of his risen body, and explained more fully both the breadth of Old Testament books that foretold his saving work and the details of his mission, which those ancient Scriptures revealed. He said:

> "Everything written about me in the Law of Moses and the Prophets and the Psalms must be fulfilled." Then he opened their minds to understand the Scriptures, and said to them, "Thus is it written, that the Christ should suffer and on the third day rise from the dead, and that repentance and forgiveness of sins should be proclaimed in his name to all nations, beginning from Jerusalem. You are witnesses of these things. And behold, I am sending the promise of my Father upon you. But stay in the city until you are clothed with power from on high." (Luke 24:44–49)

What do these almost back-to-back accounts of the risen Lord's exposition of the Scriptures teach us about the Old Testament and how to interpret it? As we reflect on the conversations in Luke 24, several truths emerge.

Jesus Connected the Whole Old Testament Canon to His Redemptive Mission

To appreciate this point, we need to understand the order of the Old Testament books as they are found in the Hebrew Scriptures, which differs somewhat from the order we find in our English versions. Our structuring of the Old Testament is derived from the Septuagint, the ancient Greek translation of the Scriptures. In our translations, we have four divisions: (1) the Pentateuch (Genesis through Deuteronomy, the "five books" of Moses); (2) the historical books (Joshua, Judges, Ruth, Samuel, Kings, Chronicles, Ezra, Nehemiah, Esther); (3) the poetical books (Job, Psalms, Proverbs, Ecclesiastes, Song of Songs); and (4) the Prophets (Isaiah through Malachi). In the Hebrew canon, however, the Scriptures are grouped into three sections:

(1) Torah (Law or Instruction) (Genesis through Deuter-onomy, the books of Moses);

(2) Prophets, which include two subdivisions: (a) "former prophets" (Joshua, Judges, Samuel, Kings); and (b) "lat-ter prophets" (Isaiah, Jeremiah, Ezekiel, and the Minor Prophets);

(3) Writings (Psalms, Proverbs, Job, Song of Songs, Ruth, Lamentations, Ecclesiastes, Esther, Daniel, Ezra-Nehemiah, Chronicles).

Now, keeping in mind the way in which first-century (and later) Jews would view the subdivisions of the Hebrew Scrip-tures, consider again the portions of the Old Testament that Jesus opened to teach the two disciples en route to Emmaus, and then the larger group later in Jerusalem. To the two Jesus expounded from "Moses and all the Prophets" the things concerning himself (Luke 24:27). Thus he took them through passages in the Pentateuch, in which Moses told of creation and the fall, human sin and the flood, Abraham and other patriarchs, the exodus from Egypt and pilgrimage through the desert, commandments pertaining to holiness and justice, the sanctuary and its sacrifices, and so on. Jesus also opened to them passages that spoke of himself in "all the Prophets." To the Jewish mind, "the Prophets" include not only the sermons and predictions of Isaiah, Ezekiel, and Hosea, but also the covenantal history of Israel's life in God's land, narrated in Joshua, Judges, Samuel, and Kings.

Although we do not know which specific passages Jesus expounded, Luke's summary suggests that he might have sketched out how the whole history of Israel—the creation of the universe, the flood, the patriarchs, Moses and the exodus, the giving of the law at Sinai, wilderness wandering, the conquest of Canaan, the chaotic years of the judges, the monarchy under Saul, David, Solomon, followed by the fracturing of the kingdom, exile, and return from exile—contained glimpses of and longings for the coming of the perfect King, the ultimate Rescuer, the faithful, covenant-keeping Israel. Then Jesus moved on to the latter prophets, perhaps Jeremiah, Joel, Micah, and Malachi, through whom God promised that he would rescue unfaithful Israel, bringing into ever-clearer focus the coming Redeemer: Immanuel, the Suffering Servant of the Lord, the son of David, the Branch who will make a new covenant, the Lord who will replace hearts of stone with hearts of flesh by his Spirit, God himself coming to his temple as a refiner's fire, his way prepared by his messenger.

Later, to the larger group that included his apostles, Jesus explained "the Law of Moses and the Prophets and the Psalms" (Luke 24:44). Again he explained our Pentateuch ("Law of Moses") and historical books and Prophets ("Prophets"); but now a third section appears: "the Psalms." The book of Psalms is the first book in "the Writings," the third division of the Hebrew Old Testament canon. It is probably mentioned in Luke's summary to indicate that this whole section of the Scriptures (wisdom books, later historical narratives, etc.) was included in the "curriculum" that Jesus taught that evening. In other words, Luke's summary is shorthand for the whole Old Testament— "from Genesis to Malachi," as we might say.

It is obvious that the New Testament focuses on Jesus. The Gospels tell the story of his birth, his ministry, and his death and resurrection. Acts relates the extension of the church through the preaching of the gospel, in the power of the Holy Spirit, whom Jesus bestowed at Pentecost. The Epistles explain the meaning of Jesus and his work of redemption. Finally, Revelation portrays the final victory of Jesus. But now we learn from Jesus himself that the whole Old Testament speaks of him as well.

So here we see the answer to the first question we posed at the beginning of the chapter: What does it mean to journey with Jesus through his Word? It means letting him teach us how to interpret the Bible. So it also means learning to see him in the Word. In other words, to combine the two ideas, it means asking Jesus to show us himself in the Bible.

Luke 24 also answers the second question: Does all of the Bible really talk about Jesus? Yes, indeed, we can definitely see every text of Scripture, from Genesis to Revelation, as a witness that points to Jesus Christ.

The Placement of These Conversations Shows Their Importance

The events recounted in Luke 24 constitute the "hinge," the crucial turning point between Jesus' ministry through his personal presence on earth, recorded in Luke's Gospel, and Jesus' ministry from heaven through his Spirit's presence in the church, described in the book of Acts. These resurrection appearances and the teaching that Jesus offers in them are the climax of "all that Jesus began to do and teach, until the day when he was taken up" to heaven (as Luke sums it up in Acts 1:1–2).

At the same time, these postresurrection, preascension Bible studies show the source of the apostles' life-transforming preaching in Acts. In Acts 1:3, we read that Jesus appeared to his apostles over forty days, "speaking about the kingdom of God." That is Luke's shorthand for these longer summaries of Jesus' instruction, recorded in the last chapter of his Gospel. His teaching prepared them for their mission as his witnesses (v. 8). In other words, Jesus' instruction in biblical interpretation, provided over that intensive forty-day period, set the stage for the apostles' preaching of Christ from the Old Testament as we find it in the pages of Acts.

Jesus Showed How Various Dimensions of His Redemptive Mission Were Foreshadowed in the Old Testament

To the downcast disciples on the road to Emmaus, Jesus said that Scripture shows that it was "necessary" for the Christ to "suffer these things" and then to enter his glory (Luke 24:26). Some years later, Peter would use the same two categories to sum up what the Spirit of Christ foretold through the Old Testament prophets: "the sufferings of Christ and the subsequent glories" (1 Peter 1:11).

Within these two general categories—suffering, followed by glory—the Old Testament reveals more specific themes and events in the life and saving mission of the Christ. Jesus expounded many of these details when he appeared to the apostles and others in Jerusalem (Luke 24:44–49). He showed them that "it is written" in Moses, the Prophets, the Psalms, and the rest of the Old Testament books:

- That the Christ would suffer;
- That he would rise from the dead on the third day;
- That repentance and forgiveness would be proclaimed in his name;
- That this proclamation would go not only to Israel, but to all other nations;
- That the Holy Spirit would empower the apostles to testify; and
- That the preachers' mission would begin from Jerusalem and spread out from there.

This shows us that to journey with Jesus through the varied terrain of his Word and the eras of redemptive history is not to strum a one-stringed guitar! Of course, Jesus' cross and resurrection take center stage in the true, historical drama of God's costly rescue enterprise. But the multidimensional effects of his redemption are reflected throughout Israel's Scriptures. When we read the Bible through the lens of Jesus Christ, we glimpse an astonishing display and array of wisdom, mercy, and power. We see how "the manifold grace of God" (1 Peter 4:10 NASB; see Eph. 3:10) radiates in all directions from the beloved eternal Son, who became the well-pleasing incarnate Son, who was rejected as the curse-bearing Son for us, and who was raised to life and now reigns in glory as the exalted Son.

We Need Jesus to Open Our Minds and Hearts

We need Jesus to open the Bible to us, and to open us up to the Bible. Luke 24 uses several words to describe the process by which Jesus disclosed the meaning of Old Testament passages. He "interpreted" to the two on the road in all the Scriptures the things concerning himself (v. 27), and they recalled how he had "opened to us the Scriptures" (v. 32). But this was not merely an intellectual communication of information.

Listen again, carefully, to Jesus' abrupt response to his fellow travelers' heartbroken confusion: "O foolish ones, and slow of heart to believe all that the prophets have spoken!" (Luke 24:25). His reaction to their dashed hopes and downcast demeanor seems insensitive and rude.

But Jesus was not going out of his way to be offensive when he called these men foolish and slow-hearted to believe God's Word. Rather, he was showing them and us that discovering each passage's link to Scripture's focal point, Christ, is not just a matter of learning a technique or following a formula, irrespective of the spiritual condition of our hearts. When we fail to see how the whole Bible focuses on Christ at its center, part of our problem—not the whole problem, but part of it—may be that our hearts are sluggish, slow, and unbelieving. Maybe we are not coming to our Bibles with the anticipation that everything between their covers is given to us by our loving Creator and Redeemer to draw our hearts more firmly to himself in confident trust, humble repentance, and grateful love. It could be that our troubling circumstances around us loom larger in our minds than the sure promises that God has spoken in his Word, as they did in the lives of Cleopas and his companion. Or maybe we are repulsed, as Simon Peter was (Matt. 16:21–23), by the pathway that Scripture lays out for the Messiah—first suffering, then glory and joy—and for those who follow the Messiah (Acts 14:22; 2 Cor. 4:17). When we have trouble seeing how the whole Bible centers on Christ, the problem may well be not in the Bible or even in our Bible-study strategies, but in ourselves.

The wonderful thing is that Jesus did not merely express frustration and rebuke over his followers' obtuseness and resistance to Christ-centered, Scripture-secured hope. The stranger kept on talking (whether they wanted him to or not). And as he talked, their hearts, previously chilled by disappointment and confusion, got warmer and warmer, to the ignition point: "Did not our hearts burn within us while he talked to us on the road, while he opened to us the Scriptures?" (Luke 24:32). Luke later describes this inner spiritual dynamic, which comes at God's initiative rather than through our mental effort, in these simple terms: Jesus "opened their minds to understand the Scriptures" (v. 45).

So here is the first key to our seeing Christ in the entire Bible: We need him to open our minds, to ignite our hearts, to take away the foolishness and sluggishness and unbelief and low expectations with which we approach his holy written Word. Since we need Jesus to do this for us, one indispensable key to journeying with Jesus through the Bible is to *pray*, to ask the Lord to open our minds and shine his light brightly into our hearts (Eph. 1:15–19). Left to yourself, you will not "get" what God intends to show you of his Son in his Word by your own research and analysis and ingenuity. Pray that as you read the Word, his Spirit will remove the veil of misunderstanding that keeps you from seeing Jesus' ever-increasing glory (2 Cor. 3:14–18). Ask "God, who said, 'Let light shine out of darkness,'" to shine with increasing radiance "in our hearts to give the light of the knowledge of the glory of God in the face of Jesus Christ" (4:6).

Now we can answer the third question from the beginning of the chapter: Why is it important to learn to journey with Jesus through his Word? First, Jesus taught his apostles to read the Word at a pivotal historical moment, between his sufferings on earth and his glories in heaven. Like them and through their writings, we must learn to read the Bible as Christ taught them to read it. Second, when Jesus opens the Scriptures and opens our minds and hearts, we discover the rich beauty, the varied dimensions, of his manifold grace. Third, seeing Jesus' glory in the Bible transforms us from the inside out, to reflect his own truth and love (2 Cor. 3:18).

Another Road, Another Heart Set Afire

Let us consider one more account recorded by Luke. It is about another Bible study conducted on another journey. In this case, it was not Jesus in person who explained the Scriptures, but his servant Philip. Yet it was the Spirit of Jesus, the Holy Spirit, who illumined both Philip and an African leader who was puzzling over a passage from the Old Testament prophets. The conversation recorded in Acts 8:26–35 gives us a taste of how the Christ-centered way of reading Scripture that Jesus taught his apostles was passed along to another generation of Christians.

The Philip in this passage is not one of the twelve apostles, but rather one of seven men chosen by the early church to care for the material needs of widows (Acts 6:1–7). When his colleague Stephen was martyred for his bold witness about Jesus, Philip and others were scattered by persecution away from Jerusalem. He ended up in the territory once occupied by the Philistines, along the Mediterranean coast.

In God's flawless planning, Philip encountered an African governmental dignitary, a eunuch who served as the secretary of the treasury for the queen of Ethiopia (the ancient Nubian kingdom located in what is now Sudan). In another divine "coincidence," the Ethiopian was reading a scroll of the prophecy of Isaiah. In an age long before the printing press, such a long scroll, copied by hand, was an expensive treasure. For a foreign dignitary to invest both the effort to travel and the expense to obtain this document shows that he had a ravenous hunger to know the true and living God, the God of Israel. This is even more remarkable because his physical condition of being a eunuch had excluded him from entering the Lord's temple in Jerusalem. Ethiopia (Nubia) was ruled by a dynasty of queens, who had male officials castrated to prevent sexual misconduct. Yet the surgery that qualified him to wield power in Ethiopia disqualified him from entering the courts of the Lord (see Deut. 23:1).

As he returned in his private coach, the eunuch was reading aloud the song of the Suffering Servant of the Lord in Isaiah 53. Philip, traveling on foot, overheard him and asked, "Do you understand what you are reading?" (Acts 8:30). With humility born of puzzlement, the eunuch replied, "How can I, unless someone guides me?" (v. 31). The Greek word translated "guides" evokes the image of one who leads another along a road, as a blind person needs a sighted person to be his guide (Matt. 15:14).

Philip did not rebuke him. Instead, he started from the Scripture that God had arranged for that very rendezvous, and he told the Ethiopian treasurer the good news about Jesus, the Lamb of God who takes away the sin of the world. When they came to water, the Ethiopian asked to receive baptism, that outward sign of the washing away of sin's defilement through faith in the Suffering Servant-Messiah. From there he went home to the queen's court full of joy, and Nubia became one of the earliest Christian communities in Africa.

I suspect that as his coach rumbled south after his baptism, the eunuch continued reading Isaiah's prophecy, but now with new eyes. If he did, he soon came to chapter 56, where he found the prediction of a coming day when God would welcome both foreigners and eunuchs into his sanctuary, to worship in the midst of the Lord's holy assembly (vv. 3–7). We know that this text was dear to Jesus, who appealed to it to explain his outrage at the greedy, commercial desecration of the temple's courts, obstructing the temple's true purpose (Mark 11:17). Through

Isaiah, the Lord had said of Gentile foreigners, "These I will bring to my holy mountain, and make them joyful in my house of prayer; . . . for my house shall be called a house of prayer for all peoples" (Isa. 56:7). Surely this African leader, previously excluded as both a foreigner and a eunuch but now welcomed by God's grace in Jesus, was a firstfruit fulfillment of Isaiah's prophecy!

The Ethiopian needed a guide, someone to lead him by the hand, as it were, through the pages of the Scriptures and to point out the landmarks and the road signs that God had installed over the centuries to keep his people facing forward, moving toward the coming of their true King and supreme Rescuer, Jesus the Messiah.

How Can We Learn to Read the Bible from Jesus?

The Ethiopian did not personally attend Jesus' forty-day crash course in biblical interpretation. Yet he did hear Jesus open the Scriptures, through Philip, who in turn had heard Peter and John and other apostles. In a similar way, we, too, can learn from the apostles' forty days of intensive Bible study with Jesus by paying attention to the way that they and the other inspired New Testament writers read the wide spectrum of Old Testament passages in light of their fulfillment in Jesus.

We don't need to envy Cleopas and his traveling companion, or Peter, Andrew, James, and John. In a sense, we also have access to those historic studies in Scripture that Jesus conducted. After all, the sermons of Peter and others in the book of Acts exhibit not only a new confidence (replacing the old discouragement) but also a new insight into Scripture and God's redemptive plan revealed in the Word. It is not too far a stretch to infer that the texts that Jesus interpreted over the forty days between his resurrection and his ascension included those to which the apostolic preachers turned as they testified to the facts and the significance of his death and his resurrection: Joel 2, Psalm 16, and Psalm 110 on the day of Pentecost (Acts 2); Isaiah 52–53, Deuteronomy 18, and Genesis 12 in Solomon's Portico (Acts 3); and so on. Moreover, the same Spirit of Christ who predicted the sufferings of Christ through the Old Testament prophets (1 Peter 1:11) later inspired the apostolic authors of the New Testament (1 Cor. 2:10–13; 2 Cor. 3:5–11; 1 Thess. 1:5; 2:13).

We have reason to read the whole New Testament as the commentary given to us by Jesus, our risen Lord, to help us grasp the message of the Old Testament as it leads us to him.

In that spirit, get in step with Jesus, and journey with him through the Bible.

Conclusion

As Cleopas and his friend journeyed with Jesus on the road to Emmaus, their Master led them through ancient Scriptures, tracing their "geography" and showing the routes that led the Christ (and his people) from suffering into glory. Later, traveling the road to Gaza, Philip guided an African dignitary along the same path from the words of the prophet Isaiah: God's well-pleasing Servant, pierced for others' offenses, has healed us by his wounds and been exalted to glory. His name is Jesus.

Cleopas saw the risen Christ and heard his voice; the Ethiopian did not. But God's Holy Spirit ignited the same flame of faith and joy in the hearts of both, as they discovered that God's words spoken centuries earlier find their focus and fulfillment in Jesus Christ. Today, through the direction that Christ's Spirit has provided through the inspired authors of the New Testament, we, too, can discover how the whole Bible leads us to Christ. As we do, we will find our sluggish, slow-to-believe hearts set ablaze with wonder and love for our Redeemer.

Review Questions

1. Explain the analogy used by the old preacher in Spurgeon's illustration to show that the whole Bible speaks of Jesus.

2. What did Jesus explain to the disciples on the way to Emmaus when he opened the Scriptures to them?

3. What does it mean to journey with Jesus through his Word?

4. How do we know that the whole Bible speaks of Jesus, according to what we learned from the passages in Luke 24? Explain the meaning of the terms "Moses," "the Prophets," and "the Psalms" in that context.

5. From the change of heart experienced by the disciples on the road to Emmaus, what have you learned about the importance of journeying with Jesus through his Word?

6. According to Luke 24:44–49, what events and truths about Jesus are written in the Old Testament?

7. What did Philip teach the Ethiopian eunuch, according to the account in Acts 8?

Questions for Reflection

1. From what you know of the Old Testament, for which books or types of Old Testament literature is the claim hardest to support that they are "united by one central

theme, a single plotline, and a unique Hero, Jesus the Messiah"? Why is this "audacious claim" so hard to believe for those parts of the Bible?

2. Why is it not enough simply to learn an interpretive technique or "key" to "open the Scriptures"? Why must we also have our minds opened, our hearts set afire, by the risen Christ? How does this happen today? What should we do to seek this opening of our minds?

3. How do you prepare to study the Scriptures?

4. Have you ever felt that your heart was "burning" as you read the Bible? How could you experience that more often?

5. What is the significance of the fact that in Acts 1:16, before the outpouring of the Holy Spirit on Pentecost, the apostle Peter interpreted the Psalms as fulfilled in the suffering of Jesus? How did Peter learn to read the Bible that way?

Exercises

As we progress through the book, we will apply the lessons of each chapter to the study of a few Bible passages, one from the Old Testament Law, one from an Old Testament historical narrative, one from the poetical books, one from the Prophets, and one from the New Testament. This will help you learn to journey with Jesus through the Bible. (In the last chapter, as our journey approaches our destination, you will make your own choice of a biblical text and apply what you have learned by tracing the route that connects it to Christ.) In this chapter, you will begin by simply noting a few thoughts regarding the following passages. What do you think they might teach us about Jesus?

- Leviticus 25:8–10 (The Year of Jubilee)
- 1 Samuel 17:38–54 (David and Goliath)
- Psalm 1 (Like a tree by the streams of water)
- Jeremiah 1:4–10 (The call of Jeremiah)
- Romans 1:16–17 (The righteous shall live by faith)

2

GETTING THE LAY OF THE LAND

The Covenant Stream That
Flows through the Bible

IN THIS CHAPTER, we will journey with Jesus all the way back to the beginning of human history, to the first chapters of the Bible. We will let him help us understand some passages in Genesis and see how they point to him. But first, let's climb to the top of a mountain to look at the whole landscape of the Bible.

From high above, we observe the hills and valleys, and we notice a stream that winds its way down to the lake in the valley. Beside the lake is a town that offers shelter from the coming storm. Although we cannot foresee the creek's every twist and turn, we know that gravity is pulling its waters down to the lake. Its flow shows the lay of the land, and we know that we want to end up where that water is heading—down to the lake and the town.

This illustrates the importance of paying attention to how a specific passage fits into the overall terrain of the Bible. For all of the Bible's diversity of speakers and actors, people and places, prose and poetry, descriptions and demands, at its heart Holy Scripture is about the relationship of God the Creator to his human creatures. The books of the Bible trace the unfolding history of that relationship:

(1) From its pristine joy at creation;
(2) Through its disruption by our fall into sin;
(3) To its restoration through God's merciful rescue, which is:
  (a) First anticipated in the promises and previews in the Old Testament;
  (b) Then accomplished by Jesus (in his obedient life, sacrificial death, and triumphant resurrection);
  (c) Now being applied to our lives by the Holy Spirit; and finally
  (d) To be consummated in the new heaven and earth.

Through all of the Bible's mountains and valleys, flatlands and rolling meadows and dense woods, "the lay of the land" is always this relationship between the personal Creator and his personal, human creatures, made in his own image.

The biblical way to say that the Bible is about the relationship of God and human beings is to say that it is about *covenant*. To get the lay of the land that shows how all roads (and even faint footpaths) lead to Scripture's metropolis—or, to shift the image slightly, to follow the current of the biblical stream as it flows toward the lake—we need to view the whole Bible as the book of the covenant, the book about the bond between our Creator-Lord and us, his creature-servants.

Jesus himself highlighted the importance of the covenant at the Last Supper, when he described his saving work in covenantal terms:

This cup that is poured out for you is the new covenant in my blood. (Luke 22:20)

In this chapter, we will deal with the following questions:

- What is a biblical covenant?
- Does the concept of the covenant flow through the whole Bible?
- How does the concept of the covenant help us understand the Scriptures?

As an example, we will analyze a passage from Genesis to see how the concept of the covenant helps us understand it.

Covenant as the Stream Flowing through Scripture

Open your Bible to the page just before Genesis 1, and then to the page just before Matthew 1. I am almost certain that on those two pages you will read the words *Old Testament* and *New Testament*. Christian readers of the Bible are so accustomed to these terms that we might skip past those "title pages" without much thought. But we need to consider where these titles came from, and what they tell us about the structure and content of God's written Word.

In our day, *testament* has legal overtones. It often appears in the phrase *last will and testament*, denoting the document by which an individual directs how his or her property is to be distributed when the person has died. To discover the full significance of this term as it appears in our Bibles, however, we need to trace its roots to the history of Bible translation.

Our English word *testament* comes from the Latin word

testamentum. Early Christian translators used *testamentum* in Latin to try to convey the sense of the New Testament Greek term *diathēkē.* The *Septuagint* (the Greek translation of the Old Testament that was used by ancient Jews and Christians) used *diathēkē* to translate the Hebrew word *berith.* Now, in the Hebrew Scriptures, a *berith* was a solemn, legal commitment between living persons—a dominant king and a weaker king (2 Chron. 16:1–4), a husband and a wife (Mal. 2:14), a father-in-law and a son-in-law (Laban and Jacob, Gen. 31:44–54), and, of course, the Lord and Israel (Ex. 24:7–8). The *berith*-maker did not have to die in order for the requirements of the *berith* to be implemented. In that sense, it was more like a political treaty between nations or marital vows or a business contract: as soon as it was ratified, it obligated the parties to keep their respective ends of the bargain.

English has another word that captures the concept that we are talking about (namely, a one-sided relationship in which the dominant party sets the terms but both parties make commitments). That word is *covenant.* So as we come to those pages just before Genesis 1 and Matthew 1, there is good reason to invest *Testament* with the fuller biblical significance that is expressed in the word *covenant.* In fact, key biblical texts, such as Jeremiah 31, actually require us to see the structure of Scripture as a whole as marked by the historical transition from an old covenant to a new covenant.

Jeremiah 31 and the Structure of the Scriptures

The basis for the age-old description of the Bible's two sections (Old Testament and New Testament) goes back to God's promise in Jeremiah 31:31–34. God spoke to his people in exile of a coming day of new beginnings—a new covenant that would not be like the bond he had made with their ancestors at Mount Sinai. Israel had violated that earlier covenant, and the people were suffering the consequences. But under the new covenant, God would write his law on the hearts of his people and forgive their sins once and for all, so that their disobedience and guilt could no longer disrupt their relationship with their covenant Lord.

Jeremiah's implication by calling the coming covenant "new" is spelled out in the New Testament: the bond that God had made with the Israelites through Moses after rescuing them from Egypt was the "old covenant." Quoting Jeremiah 31:31–34, the epistle to the Hebrews comments: "In speaking of a new covenant, [God] makes the first one obsolete" (Heb. 8:13). The apostle Paul makes the same point in 2 Corinthians 3, where he says that he and other preachers of the gospel have now been appointed and qualified by God to be "ministers of a new covenant" (2 Cor. 3:3, 6). Then Paul goes on to describe the weekly reading of the law of Moses in Jewish synagogues as the reading of "the old covenant" (vv. 14–15). Paul and the author to the Hebrews are affirming the fact that Jesus himself initiated the new covenant. As mentioned previously, in instituting the Lord's Supper the evening before his sacrifice, Jesus spoke of the wine: "This cup that is poured out for you is the new covenant in my blood" (Luke 22:20; see the similar wording of 1 Cor. 11:25).

The Components of Biblical Covenants

What does the Bible mean when it uses *covenant* to characterize the relationship of the Creator with his creatures, and specifically with human beings? The covenants in the Bible differ in various details, but this working description captures the main features:

The Lord's covenant with his human servants is a bond of interpersonal commitment involving exclusive loyalty, sovereignly instituted by the Lord, expressed through their mutual obligations, and enforced by life or death consequences.[1]

Let's examine these components one by one. First, a covenant is a committed relationship, a relationship of exclusive loyalty. Between the Lord and his people the bond is intimate and affectionate, so it is compared to marriage. As a husband who loves his wife passionately and expects her affection and fidelity in return, so the Lord is jealous for his people to love and trust him alone, not wandering after any other god. This bond is also legal and structured, so some biblical covenants have formal features that make them resemble international treaties among ancient Near Eastern monarchs. At the core of God's covenant with us is his demand for exclusive love, loyalty, and trust. He pledges his allegiance—he "plights his troth," as wedding services once said—to his people, and in return he expects them to love and obey him—and him alone—as their Lord and Protector.

Second, these bonds are sovereignly instituted by the Lord. They are not negotiated contracts between equals, but bonds between unequals (Lord and servant, Creator and creature, Sovereign and subordinate). Covenants are imposed by the Lord, whose powerful prior actions have made the covenant bond possible and created its context. He exercises his right to set the standards and conditions. Covenants begin with what God has done (creation, exodus, cross); and from God's action flow the motive, rationale, and form for our response as his servants.

---

1. Expanded from O. Palmer Robertson, *The Christ of the Covenants* (Phillipsburg, NJ: Presbyterian and Reformed, 1980), 3–15. Robertson states concisely on page 4: "A covenant is a bond in blood sovereignly administered."

Third, the covenant loyalty between the Lord and his servants is more than emotional attachment. It is to be lived out in action, in the keeping of mutual obligations.

Finally, there are consequences that will result, depending on the parties' performance of their respective obligations. In the Lord's covenants with his people, of course there can be no question about the Lord's faithfulness to fulfill his commitments (although his people sometimes have their doubts, Ps. 89:38–51). The Lord's very identity sets the norm for truth and trustworthiness, and his power and wisdom are boundless, so it is impossible for him to lie (Heb. 6:18) or to fail to deliver on what he has promised. On the other hand, the Bible is realistic about the possibility that the covenant servants will fail to keep their obligations, and thereby incur disastrously negative consequences.

The sober reality is that only one covenant Servant in all of human history actually kept his commitment flawlessly—and he, Jesus, was the Lord who became Servant both to obey and to suffer the consequences that his people deserved. Jesus came to keep the servant's obligation of loving, obedient loyalty on our behalf, and so to share with us the reward of eternal life, God's favor that his sinless perfection deserves. He also came to endure, on our behalf, the death that our own disloyal rebellion deserves, setting us free from that cursed consequence. Jesus' mission as covenant-keeper and curse-bearer in our place is the amazing grace that lies at the foundation of the covenant of grace.

These components can often be seen in the covenantal arrangements throughout the Bible. For example, when you look carefully, you'll see that the whole book of Deuteronomy has a structure that reflects these components: (1) the commitment of exclusive loyalty (Deut. 6:4–5), (2) its sovereign inauguration based on the Lord's rescue in the exodus and his preservation in the wilderness, (3) the obligations given in the law on Sinai (chaps. 1–5), along with the implementation in concrete commands (chaps. 6–26), and (4) its consequences (chaps. 27–30).

The Parties to the Biblical Covenants

We have seen that biblical covenants bind two parties, the Lord and his servant people, in a committed relationship of loyal love. The Lord and servant have contrasting and complementary roles. When we pay attention to how Jesus Christ fulfills the Lord's and the servant's roles, two wonderful things result. First, we begin to appreciate what the apostle Paul means when he describes Jesus as the "one mediator between God and men" (1 Tim. 2:5) and what Hebrews means in calling Jesus "the mediator of a new covenant" (Heb. 9:15; 12:24; see also 8:6). Christ is the one and only divine and human person, whose unique mission is to maintain the covenant bond between the holy God and his unholy people.

Second, we are alerted to the perspective that every biblical instance of the Lord's role and the servant's role in the covenant bond between God and his people reflects, in one way or another, the ministry of Christ, who holds the faithful Lord and his wayward people together by fulfilling both the Lord's commitment and the servant's commitment—completely and perfectly.

The Lord takes initiative to institute the covenant bond. Through his prior acts of creation and rescue, the Lord sets the scene for the covenant and establishes his servants' dependence on and obligation to him (Gen. 2:5–15; Ex. 20:1–2). Through his promises and commands, he sovereignly sets its terms (Gen. 2:16–17; Ex. 20:3–17). He provides for his servants' needs as

30

the loving Husband of his bride (Jer. 2:2–3; Ezek. 16; Hos. 2; Isa. 54:5–8). As the vigilant Shepherd of his flock, he protects them from enemy attack (Ezek. 34:11–24). And because he is Lord, God also exerts his authority to judge, rewarding faithfulness and punishing rebellion (Josh. 7; Isa. 2:2–4; 3:13–15; Joel 3:12–16).

In the fullness of time, Jesus came as covenant Lord, to keep God's every promise (2 Cor. 1:19–20) and to accomplish the Lord's every role as Sovereign Creator, Rescuer, Provider, Protector, and Judge. He was the divine Agent of the original creation (John 1:1–4; Col. 1:15–17; Heb. 1:1–3), and by his Holy Spirit he brings us to life in the new creation (1 Cor. 15:45). Jesus is the "I Am" who came to rescue his enslaved people (Ex. 3:7–14; John 8:51–58). He is the Lord who stills the raging seas to save his own (Ps. 107:23–32; Mark 4:35–41). He provides for his bride as our generous Husband (Mark 2:19–20; Eph. 5:25–32). He protects his sheep, even laying down his life for theirs (John 10:1–18). Christ comes as Commander, demanding exclusive loyalty (Matt. 10:37–39) and equating love for him with obedience to his commands (John 14:21–24). Finally, Jesus exerts his sovereign authority in rendering just judgment (John 5:30) and separating the nations as a shepherd distinguishes blessed sheep from rejected goats (Matt. 25:31–46).

The servant's role is to respond to the Lord's initiative with trusting dependence, wholehearted loyalty, and unswerving obedience. In covenant with the Creator, the servant enjoys a *privileged preeminence*, receives abundant *provision*, and undergoes a *probation* of his faithfulness, which issues in the *product* of that testing process, either blessing or curse.

In the beginning, God created human beings in his own image and in covenant with himself, giving them dominion over other creatures (Gen. 1:26–30). This privileged identity with and relationship to the Creator bestowed on the servant a unique honor, as the servant submitted to his Lord. Later, God's covenant imparted to Israel a privileged status among all the peoples of the earth (Ex. 19:5–6; Amos 3:1–2). The Lord provided for his servant in lavish generosity. This provision is seen in Eden, in God's encouragement to enjoy fruit from every tree but one (Gen. 2:8–17). For his servant Israel, the Lord provided a promised land flowing with milk and honey, lush with produce from heaven's rainfall (Deut. 11:8–15).

Yet as satisfying as both Eden and the promised land were, they were also the arenas in which the loyalty and submission of the servant would be tested, put on probation. Would Adam and Eve heed God's Word or the tempter's lie, eating from the one and only tree forbidden them (Gen. 2:17; 3:1–7)? Would the Israelites serve the Lord alone in the land he had given them, or would they bow their hearts to the impotent gods of the defeated Canaanites (Deut. 8:11–20)? The probation would issue in contrasting products, diametrically opposite outcomes: well-being and life in the joy of the Lord's presence for steadfast obedience, or anguish and utter destruction in banishment for treasonous rebellion (Gen. 3:22–24; Deut. 28). The story line of the whole Old Testament, from Eden to exile (and a disappointing return from exile), documents the miserable failures of God's covenant servants and the dire product of their disloyalty. As Israel's Scriptures draw to a close, God's guilty servants are left longing for a loyal Servant who would keep faithfulness and achieve blessedness where they (like all of us) had failed.

In the fullness of time, Jesus came as the Lord's perfect covenant Servant, to keep every commandment and to earn every blessing that Adam, and Israel, and you and I have forfeited through our treason against our Creator and King. His privilege and preeminence are unparalleled, for he is the man who not only bears but actually is the image of God, supreme Ruler as the last and greatest Adam (Col. 1:15–18; 1 Cor. 15:45). He entered not a world of pristine peace and abundance, but one of waste and want and threat, undergoing the first assault of his probation not in a lush garden but in a barren desert, surrounded by wild animals (Mark 1:12–13). God's provision for this perfect Servant was not lavish physical abundance, but the "food" of doing his Father's will (John 4:34), employing the body prepared for him to achieve his mission of sacrificial suffering (Heb. 10:5–10).

On the earthly battlefield littered with the casualties of covenant violations, this Servant sustained lifelong probation, his devotion and allegiance tested in every respect, and he sustained every trial with wholehearted, unflinching, utterly sinless fidelity to God the Lord (Heb. 4:14–16; 5:7–10). Yet this flawless covenant Servant, whose unblemished purity deserved only the blessedness of eternal life, did in fact die. The cursed product of failed probation, which Adam and Israel and we deserve, the faithful Servant received—and willingly embraced (Gal. 3:13–14). He did so to absorb others' cursedness and to impart to them his own well-earned blessedness. In the end, fittingly, death—that ultimate covenant curse—had no right to hold him in its grasp (Acts 2:22–32). God vindicated, exalted, and glorified his well-pleasing Servant Jesus (Isa. 52:13–15; Acts 3:13–16).

This all-too-brief survey of the roles of covenant Lord and covenant Servant, and of how Christ fulfills both roles completely, whets our appetite and alerts our senses to discover how the Bible's covenantal lay of the land draws us inexorably to him, the only Mediator between God and men, the unique Mediator of the covenant of grace.

Now, having glimpsed the components and parties of biblical

covenants, let's look upstream from the lake to find the tributaries that pour into it along the way. Let's take a quick look at key references to the covenant in the Old Testament, eventually going all the way back to the beginning.

Key Covenants

Having explained the components and parties of biblical covenants, we will now examine the extent to which the covenant concept flows across the entire terrain of God's Word. We will walk upstream, tracing the current backward in time to where it all begins. We will discover that at history's dawn the Creator engaged Adam and Eve in a covenant that would test their trust and loyalty. They failed that test, and the results were horrific. But the Lord embraced them in a different kind of covenant, a covenant of grace in which he himself would provide what they lacked, to maintain their relationship and restore their brokenness. There is one main covenant of grace, but God made covenants with different people along the way, highlighting distinct aspects of that overarching covenant. Each of these is like a tributary flowing into the same stream. What unique aspect does each one contribute?

David

God made a covenant with David (around 1000 B.C.), promising to establish his descendants as a permanent dynasty to rule over Israel.

> You have said, "I have made a covenant with my chosen one;
>   I have sworn to David my servant:
> 'I will establish your offspring forever,
>   and build your throne for all generations.'" (Ps. 89:3–4)

This promise was made to David through the prophet Nathan (2 Sam. 7:12–16). This stage highlights the aspects of sovereign rule, military defense, and wise justice. By keeping his commitment to maintain David's offspring on his royal throne, God would give his people a Monarch who would administer God's own rule, protection, and equity. The final fulfillment is in Christ, the greatest descendant of David. (See Luke 1:31–33; Heb. 1:8–9.)

Moses

Moving upstream, several centuries earlier in history, we reach Mount Sinai. The Ten Commandments given to Moses in Exodus 20 exhibit the form of a covenant, showing that God was making a covenant with Israel through him. First, like the treaties that the kings of Israel's neighbors in the ancient Near East made with other kings in the region, God's covenant treaty with Israel begins with a little history of what the Lord has done to show his commitment to his covenant servant people by rescuing and protecting them from their enemies.

Second, the mutual obligations between the Lord and his servant people come to expression in the Ten Commandments, both in God's promises and, obviously, in his commands. The third component of covenants is consequences. Faithfulness brings blessing, but treason brings curse. This covenant highlights the obligations of the subordinate people of God as they express their loyalty.

The exodus that set the Israelites free from centuries of slavery in Egypt and brought them to God's mountain in the wilderness was the result of the Lord's "remembering" and keeping his promises to their ancestors, the patriarchs Abraham, Isaac, and Jacob. "And God heard their groaning, and God remembered his covenant with Abraham, with Isaac, and with Jacob" (Ex. 2:24). Let's continue to work our way back in time toward the beginning.

Abraham

Several centuries before Moses and the exodus, God made a covenant with Abraham, promising the aged, childless nomad that one day his children would be as countless as the stars in the sky, and that they would eventually enjoy a land to call home (Gen. 15:18). (At the end of this chapter, as we put into practice this "lay of the land" perspective, we will examine the bizarre ratification ceremony by which God sealed his covenant commitment to Abraham.) The Lord also established a covenant sign, circumcision, which was to be applied to each male in Abraham's household, both sons and slaves (Gen. 17). In fact, those not circumcised were to be excluded from the community of the Lord's covenant with Abraham.

So God's covenant with Abraham exhibited the covenant components that we have discussed—God's sovereign initiation, exclusive interpersonal commitment, mutual obligations (the Lord's promises primarily, but also Abraham's response of trust, displayed in action), and ultimate consequences. Centuries before Moses, the Lord's covenant commitment to Abraham set the context for Israel's release from Egypt and consecration as the Lord's treasured people at Sinai. This covenant highlights both God's promise of loyalty and his expectation of faith on the part of his people.

Noah

Even earlier, after God's floodwaters purged the ancient world of human evil run rampant, the Lord made a covenant with Noah and his family and all other living things, designating his rainbow in the clouds as a sign of his promise not to use water to wash the world clean of human filth ever again (Gen. 9:9–17). In this covenant, the Creator's commitment embraced more than a particular individual or family or national group. As supreme Judge, he promised to withhold his final judgment for a time, to sustain the orderly succession of seasons. He made that promise to the whole order of living beings, human and animal, on earth.

This blessing of the orderly variation of sunshine and rain, warmth and cold, would not be a "consequence" dependent on creatures' fulfilling their covenant obligations. Rather, the Lord of the covenant secured it by his unilateral promise. His covenant commitment to all creatures on earth established an ongoing, stable global context in which he would pursue his special, redemptive covenant agenda for his special people, set apart by his sovereign grace, as we see in Abraham's life. God's gracious patience and sovereign protection are highlighted in this covenant.

Adam and Eve

Although the earliest appearances of the word *covenant* are in the narrative about Noah (Gen. 6:18 and repeatedly in Gen. 9), it would be premature to conclude from the absence of the word that God had no covenant relationship with human beings before the flood. For one thing, God's words to Noah, after the floodwaters had receded, echo God's words to the first man and woman at the very dawn of history: "Be fruitful and multiply and fill the earth. . . . Every moving thing that lives shall be food for you. And as I gave you the green plants, I give you everything" (9:1–3). This echo raises the intriguing possibility that God's original relationship with the first man and woman, Adam and Eve, was in fact a covenant without the label. This is the spring from which the covenant stream begins to flow.

As tantalizingly brief as the account of the creation and commissioning of the first human beings is in Genesis 1–2, do we see indications that their relationship with their Creator exhibited the components that we have seen converging to define biblical covenants?

(1) Was their relationship with their Creator sovereignly initiated by him? Absolutely! He not only made them, but also engaged them through words by which he both empowered and obligated them:

> And God blessed them. And God said to them, "Be fruitful and multiply and fill the earth and subdue it, and have dominion over the fish of the sea and over the birds of the heavens and over every living thing that moves on the earth." And God said, "Behold, I have given you every plant yielding seed that is on the face of all the earth, and every tree with seed in its fruit. You shall have them for food." (Gen. 1:28–29)

(2) Was their relationship to be a commitment of exclusive loyalty? Indeed, they were to believe God's words implicitly and to base their decisions on those words, even when Satan, speaking through a serpent, invited them to doubt both their generous Lord's motives and his veracity (Gen. 2:15–17; 3:1–5).

(3) Were there mutual obligations? The presence of the Tree of Life in God's garden symbolized his freely made promise of abundant life in his favor and presence forever (Gen. 2:9; 3:22). As his servants, Adam and Eve were certainly obligated to obey both his positive commands to work the earth and rule other creatures and his negative prohibition against eating from the Tree of the Knowledge of Good and Evil.

(4) Were there consequences? Disastrously, yes. God had announced beforehand that death would ensue if the man and

woman disregarded his word: "in the day that you eat of [the Tree of the Knowledge of Good and Evil] you shall surely die" (Gen. 2:17). So our first parents' unbelief and rebellion brought disruption and shame to their relationship with their Creator, death to themselves and all their children, disorder to their relation to each other, and frustration to their tasks (3:8–12, 16–19).

All the covenant components were there, so it seems that at the very beginning God created Adam and Eve to be in covenant with him. That, in fact, is what is implied in a striking comparison drawn by the later prophet Hosea, who compared Israel's rebellion and violation of the covenant at Sinai with Adam's first sin in eating the forbidden fruit: "But like Adam they transgressed the covenant; there they dealt faithlessly with me" (Hos. 6:7).

Of course, this earliest covenant does not include all the detailed rituals and documents that would be associated with later covenants. In later covenants, for instance, animal sacrifices and blood symbolized the dreadful consequences that would ensue if the covenant servant were to break faith with his Lord (Ex. 24:4–8; Jer. 34:18–20). (We will revisit the significance of these rituals at the end of this chapter, using the covenant theme to understand a specific Old Testament passage, Genesis 15.) The absence of bloodshed in the institution of this covenant of creation demonstrates the most dramatic difference between it and the covenant of grace (in its various administrations) that follows it. In the beginning, the covenant in Eden required our original parents to respond to God's generous provision with their own flawless loyalty and obedience. Since they fell, our only hope for escape from judgment and for restoration to God's favor lies in the flawless loyalty and obedience—and the substitutionary suffering—of another covenant Representative (as we will soon see).

Despite the differences in covenant conditions, as the

prophet Hosea looks all the way back to the beginning and then to Sinai in the less-distant past, he sees that his Israelite kinfolk are fallen, traitorous children of Adam, and that like their father they have broken the Lord's covenant. That bad news implies that when God made the man and woman in his own image, the committed relationship that he established with them was a covenant.

The Protestant pastors who gathered in Westminster Abbey in the 1640s to formulate a fresh summary of the Bible's teaching came to the same conclusion that we have reached:

> The first covenant made with man was a covenant of works, wherein life was promised to Adam; and in him to his posterity, upon condition of perfect and personal obedience. (WCF 7.2)

Now, physical death did not befall Adam and Eve at the very moment of their rebellion, although seeds of guilt and shame had been sown that would eventually produce a bitter harvest of pain and destruction. Clearly, Adam and Eve's original relationship with God—their covenant of complete commitment to and communion with their Creator—had been shattered. Would it be replaced by a hopeless stretch of ongoing existence, disconnected from the Lord who had given them life, until they finally succumbed to death and decay in the dust? Surprisingly, no. Immediately after Adam and Eve's fall into sin, Genesis describes God's establishing of a new and different kind of relationship, a "covenant of grace," as the pastors at Westminster called it:

> Man, by his fall, having made himself incapable of life by that covenant, the Lord was pleased to make a second, commonly called the covenant of grace; wherein he freely offereth unto

sinners life and salvation by Jesus Christ; requiring of them faith in him, that they may be saved, and promising to give unto all those that are ordained unto eternal life his Holy Spirit, to make them willing, and able to believe. (WCF 7.3)

This time, the promise of eternal life in joyful communion with the Creator would not depend on the first Adam's performance of "perfect and personal obedience" (WCF 7.2). Instead, it would depend on the perfect, personal obedience of a second Adam, Jesus Christ, which would then be bestowed as a free gift, unearned and undeserved, on guilty sinners who simply have faith in Christ. In this covenant the Lord binds himself to bless his guilty but trusting servants despite their infidelity, on the basis of a Substitute's covenant-keeping, graciously credited to those who, left to themselves, would be liable only to covenant curse. Was the assembly at Westminster right to hear, amid the wreckage of Genesis 3, hints of a restored relationship, sovereignly initiated and defined by God, entailing exclusive loyalty and commitments spelled out in mutual obligations, with consequences to follow? Yes!

Even though we do not see in Genesis 3 all the details that appear in later covenant-making rituals, we do hear God committing himself by a promise to separate Eve from her lethal alliance with the enemy, Satan, and ultimately to destroy that enemy (3:15). And we see God covering Adam and Eve's shame through bloodshed, the death of animals with whose skins God clothed them (v. 21). This different type of covenant appears in seed form in Genesis 3:15, which students of Scripture have often called the *protoevangelium*, the "first gospel":

I will put enmity between you and the woman,
    and between your offspring and her offspring;

> he shall bruise your head,
> and you shall bruise his heel.

God addresses these words to Satan, the archliar and archmurderer, who spoke through the serpent and lured Eve (and her husband with her) into his lie and so into guilt and death. Yet in cursing the evil tempter, God implicitly promised rescue to those who had let themselves be duped by the devil's lies. In fact, this first postfall covenant, brief as it is, brings into view the participation of both parties to the covenant, Lord and servant, in undoing the damage done through Adam's failure. At this early stage, the wording is very general: "I will put enmity between you [Satan/the serpent] and the woman, and between your offspring [the enemy's allies down through the generations] and her offspring [Eve's descendants, ultimately focused in a single Descendant]; he [that singular Descendant] shall bruise your head, and you shall bruise his heel."

Entailed in this terse curse on the evil one is the announcement that the bringing of redemption to mankind is both God's gift and man's accomplishment—but only one Man could do it. We see God's initiative in his promise, "I will put enmity between [the serpent] and the woman." The Lord will not leave Eve a guilt-ridden and helpless captive in thrall to her deceiver and destroyer. But we also see a crucial role for the woman's offspring, a human being who will be a faithful covenant Servant, who through his own suffering (having his heel bruised) will crush the evil one's power (bruise Satan's head).

God's covenants with Adam and Eve before and after their fall into sin explain the comparison and contrast between Adam and Christ that Paul draws in Romans 5 and 1 Corinthians 15. Genesis 3:15 is God's hint that, though Jesus the second Adam (the covenant-keeping Adam) would not appear in history for many centuries, his eventual arrival was sure and his victory over Satan secure. The first Adam, choosing and acting on behalf of all his natural children as our covenant representative, plunged us all into condemnation and the sentence of death. The last Adam, already promised in that tiny seed of hope implied in God's sentence of doom on the devil, would arise in due time not only to endure the poisonous curse that our breach deserved (having his heel bruised) but also to keep the covenant commitments that neither our father Adam nor we could keep.

In summary, there are two different covenants with Adam and Eve: one before the fall, and one after. The first emphasizes the obligation of total obedience, filling the earth, administering creation, and sustaining the test of the Tree of the Knowledge of Good and Evil. The second emphasizes the grace of God in his promise to send a descendant of Eve who would gain the victory.

In the opening chapters of Genesis, we discover the fountain from which the covenant waters begin to flow. The pastors gathered at Westminster were right to see the whole history of humanity's relationship with our Maker—the whole story of the Bible—as a landscape watered by the same stream of the covenant, from the first covenant of works that Adam broke until the covenant of grace that Jesus kept on believers' behalf. The grace of God is the water itself that gives life to everything in the land.

Conclusion

How does the covenant concept inform our grasp of God's Word? All of Scripture is related to the covenant, because it is all about our relationship to God as his personal image-bearers and about our rescue and restoration to that high calling through the salvation achieved by Christ. Every page contains the drama

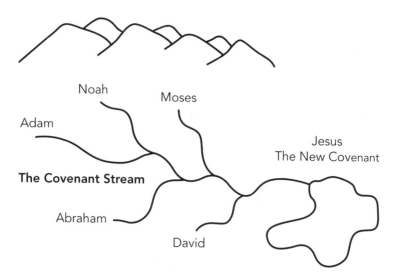

Fig. 2.1. The Lay of the Land

of the historical outworking of God's redemptive plan. If God's people are kept in slavery in Egypt, they will not inherit the promised land. If God's people are destroyed, the line of descendants leading to the Messiah is broken, and there will be no Savior and no salvation. Any story of conflict and victory, any event of captivity and deliverance, any drama of oppression and liberation reflects the underlying drama of the history of salvation. But the fact that God has made an oath to keep his covenant promises assures us that the plan of redemption will be perfectly accomplished.

In later chapters, we will notice ways in which, by virtue of their distinctive roles and responsibilities, Israel's official leaders—prophets, priests, kings, sages, judges—tended either to reproduce Adam's covenant failure or to preview, in finite and flawed ways, Christ's complete and flawless covenant faithfulness. Here we can observe that it is also true for every rank-and-file Israelite (or foreigner) who appears on the pages of Scripture that he or she (like each of us) stands related to God by way of covenant. The New England Primer taught children in the American colonies not only the alphabet but also sound biblical truth when it introduced the letter *A* with the couplet: "In Adam's fall / We sinned all." No person whom we meet in the Bible (or, for that matter, in our everyday lives) enjoys an independent life, utterly unrelated to the God who made him or her. Every natural child of Adam (and that is every one of us) is implicated in our ancestor's violation of that pristine covenant of works at history's dawn. Given the opportunity, every one of us consequently follows his lead in breaching, again and again, the bond that should have linked us to the Lord in the closest of interpersonal communion. The Bible's every record of human sin, whether "large" or "small" in our eyes, compounds the indictment of our ingrate race's defiance of the Lord whose friendship is life and our preference for the lie that breeds nothing but death. So every page of Scripture that speaks of human failure and faithlessness whets our hearts' appetite for the coming of the woman's offspring, who would love and serve the Lord with heart, soul, strength, and mind.

On the other hand, every figure in Scripture's pages who maintains loyalty and keeps commitments, however fleetingly, gives a glimpse of paradise lost, of the image of God that once reflected the Creator in untarnished radiance but has since suffered distortion and defilement. Every truthful word and trustworthy deed produced by Adam's morally mottled children also gives glimpses of two rays of hope: First, Eve's very flawed offspring down through the generations, distinguished from the serpent's offspring (Isaac vs. Ishmael, Jacob vs. Esau, David vs. Saul, etc.), point our hopes ahead to the final arrival of Eve's flawless offspring, Jesus. Second, the glimmers of covenant faithfulness that make their way to the surface in the lives of

Old and New Testament believers, damaged though they still are, give evidence of a revitalization project that God's gracious Spirit has set in motion deep within them.

So when we see in Scripture scenes of other covenant relationships that function somewhat as they should—exclusive commitment expressed in promises and commands kept, and so yielding interpersonal delight—then every such scene should lift our minds and hearts to appreciate the redemptive bond that is the template for all such creaturely replicas. When a husband such as Hosea loves and goes on loving a wife who scorns his love, he becomes a reflection of the heavenly Husband who pursues his unfaithful bride and will not let her (us) go. When Israel celebrates a royal wedding (Ps. 45), the beauty and joy of both bride and groom offer glimpses of the consummation of God's covenant with his beloved people. The friendship of Jonathan, the royal prince who gladly risked his life and relinquished his throne to David, the man of God's choosing, displays the costliness of covenant commitment. Such selfless devotion whets our soul's longing for a friend who loves with such constancy and commitment. The golden covenant thread interwoven throughout the tapestry of Scripture leads us to Christ. The mountain stream of covenant motifs shows us the lay of the land, how everything in biblical history, law, wisdom, prophecy, and more slopes and flows toward Jesus, the reservoir of God's glory and grace.

As we read a passage, we need to find its place in the flow of the covenant stream, its unique period in the history of redemption. It is especially important to distinguish between the old covenant and the new covenant. When we cross over into the New Testament, God manifests his grace in new ways, the law is written on our hearts, and the application of the Old Testament law changes.

Putting It into Practice: Fire between the Carcasses (Genesis 15:7–21)

Let's return to the time of Abraham, a few chapters downstream from the garden of Eden. Genesis 15 narrates a strange covenant-ratification ceremony. Although God had already made great promises to Abraham, here for the first time we read, "On that day the LORD made a covenant with Abram" (15:18). God had previously called Abraham to travel from Mesopotamia "to the land that I will show you" and promised to bless Abraham and to make him a means of blessing to "all the families of the earth" (12:1–3). Upon his arrival in the promised land, Abraham received God's promise that it would one day belong to "your offspring" (v. 7). Yet when God again spoke in Genesis 15:1, Abraham was still childless. In response to Abraham's complaint, God promised descendants as countless as the stars in the night sky. Abraham "believed the LORD," yet still he wondered, "O Lord God, how am I to know that I shall possess" the land (15:6, 8)?

To confirm his promises of offspring and land, the Lord instructed Abraham to make preparations for a solemn rite of covenant ratification. Abraham was to slay a heifer, a goat, a ram, and two birds, cut the carcasses of the larger animals in half, and arrange the bloody pieces in two rows on the ground, creating a gruesome corridor of death (Gen. 15:9–10).

This is the ancient ritual referred to centuries later by the prophet Jeremiah (Jer. 34:18–20). In Jeremiah's day, the leaders and people of Judah had entered a covenant with the Lord by dividing a slain calf in two and passing between the split halves of its carcass. (This could be why the Hebrew Scriptures speak of "cutting" a covenant in Genesis 15, Jeremiah 34, and elsewhere.) By chopping animal carcasses in two and walking between the bloody pieces, Jeremiah's contemporaries had said, in effect,

"We promise to free our Israelite slaves, as God's law requires. If we fail to keep our commitment, may we be cut into pieces like this calf and made carrion for birds of prey." Those who passed between the carcasses were sealing their word with their blood, placing their lives on the line. In a similar rite at Sinai, the splashing of the sacrificial blood on the Lord's altar and on the Lord's people delivered the same graphic message: as the Lord sealed his promises with his very life, so his people also swore their allegiance on their very lives (Ex. 24:3–8). Woe be to either party, Lord or servant, should he prove false!

In view of all that the Bible reveals about the utter faithfulness of God the Lord and the instability of sinful covenant servants such as Abraham, we would anticipate that in Genesis 15, even though the issue is the reliability of God's promises, Abraham should be the one to walk through those gruesome tokens of covenant curse. After all, it is Abraham who shaded the truth not once but twice, fearing human sheiks more than the Sovereign Lord who had called his name (Gen. 12:11–20; 20:1–18). Instead, however, we read that "a deep sleep fell on Abram." As he lay sedated, "a smoking fire pot and a flaming torch" (showing God's glorious presence) passed through the corpses of the sacrificed animals (15:12, 17). The Lord himself—the God of truth who sets the standard for truth, the ever-living God who cannot die—secured his word with his life, assuring his servant of his resolute commitment to fulfill all that he had promised: countless descendants like the starry sky, and a land to call home.

Later, God would reaffirm his commitment to Abraham in the words of an oath: "By myself I have sworn, . . . I will surely bless you, and I will surely multiply your offspring as the stars of heaven and as the sand that is on the seashore" (Gen. 22:16–17). Among ancient pagans, to swear an oath was to invoke the gods as witnesses of a covenant and enforcers of its commitments.

For Abraham, the Lord "swore by himself," summoning himself (since there is no deity as mighty as he) to inflict the curse on himself if he should fail to keep his commitments to Abraham. This is why Hebrews 6:13–18 says that God secured his promise to Abraham by two unchangeable things—first, his word of promise, and then the oath by which he bound his own life to the promise—to give Abraham strong encouragement to hold fast to God's word of commitment.

This is the meaning of the strange covenant-ratification ritual of Genesis 15: The Lord who has every right to demand our unwavering trust and complete devotion binds himself in covenant to servants whose faith and faithfulness are flawed and fluctuating. His commitment to bestow blessing on those who deserve covenant curse is sealed not only by his ever-reliable word but also by his invincible life.

Notice the surprising way that Jesus meets us in this bizarre event, in which the Lord's servant Abraham sleeps as the Lord puts his own life in jeopardy. In the fullness of time, this gracious and faithful covenant Lord would in fact endure his own curse, not because he had failed to keep his word but precisely in order to keep his commitment to unfaithful people like us. Only by absorbing the curse that we had earned for ourselves when we defied his authority could he justly bestow blessing on all who, like Abraham, cling to him in dependent trust. Later in the books of Moses, we read that hanging an executed lawbreaker's body on a tree signaled his cursedness before God (Deut. 21:23). That is precisely the way that Jesus was executed; and the form of his exposure in death was not lost on Paul, who applied this Deuteronomy text to Christ's cross:

> Christ redeemed us from the curse of the law by becoming a curse for us—for it is written, "Cursed is everyone who is

hanged on a tree"—so that in Christ Jesus the blessing of Abraham might come to the Gentiles, so that we might receive the promised Spirit through faith. (Gal. 3:13–14)

So the covenant that God cut with Abraham graphically foreshadows the ultimate price that the covenant Lord would pay in order to spare his curse-deserving servants and so to keep his promise to bestow, in place of the wrath we deserve, the indescribable blessing of life in his friendship and favor forever.

Review Questions

1. Where did we get the titles of the two divisions of our Bible—*Old Testament* and *New Testament*? What does this reveal about the lay of the land for the terrain of God's Word, from Genesis to Revelation?
2. What imagery is used in this chapter to illustrate the fact that the covenant concept unites all of Scripture? How does it relate to our "journeying" motif?
3. What is a biblical covenant? Describe each aspect of the definition given in the chapter. That is, what are the components of a covenant?
4. Who are the two parties of biblical covenants, and what are their respective roles? How does Jesus fulfill each role perfectly and completely?
5. What passage in Jeremiah reveals the blessings of the new covenant? What key changes does it say that the new covenant will bring?
6. What New Testament passages mentioned in this chapter also refer to the new covenant?
7. Give biblical evidence that the concept of the covenant flows through all of Scripture. Describe each Old

Testament covenant that forms a tributary to the larger stream of the covenant of grace, and mention the aspect that each one highlights.

8. How does the concept of the covenant help us understand the Scriptures?

9. How do God's words of judgment to the serpent (Satan) in Genesis 3:15 hint at features of a "covenant of grace" that God had prepared for fallen humans like Adam and Eve, like us?

10. How did the strange ritual of Genesis 15:9–21—the flaming torch that passed between pieces of slain animals, as Abraham was in a deep sleep—answer Abraham's question: "O Lord God, how am I to know that I shall possess [this land]?" What does this rite reveal about the Lord's commitment to keep his oath to those who trust him?

Questions for Reflection

1. When you approach the Bible as a book about God's relationship with us, his human image-bearers (not merely a handbook of doctrinal concepts or ethical instruction, though it reveals both inerrant truth and authoritative norms), how should that influence your purposes and expectations in reading and studying it?

2. How did this chapter help you see the unity of the whole Bible? How would you describe its main message to someone who asks you what it's all about?

3. What would you say to someone who thinks that the Bible is full of contradictions because it is written over so many years by so many different authors?

Exercises

Consider the same passages we used for the exercises in the previous chapter. Note the covenant period that each one fits into (Adam and Eve, Noah, Moses, Abraham, David, or the new covenant). Write down your thoughts about what each passage teaches regarding the covenant of grace and about salvation.

- Leviticus 25:8–10 (The Year of Jubilee)
- 1 Samuel 17:38–54 (David and Goliath)
- Psalm 1 (Like a tree by the streams of water)
- Jeremiah 1:4–10 (The call of Jeremiah)
- Romans 1:16–17 (The righteous shall live by faith)

3

"YOU ARE HERE"

Discover Where You Are and
Use the Bible Itself to Find Your Way

IN THE FIRST chapter, we joined Jesus and two of his disciples on a journey that was both short and long. In geography, the distance between Jerusalem and Emmaus is short, only seven miles, or eleven kilometers—a few hours' walk. But along the way, Jesus led them on a long trek through the ancient Word of God, from the books of Moses to those written by prophets centuries later. All along the way, in every text he touched, Jesus pointed out "the things concerning himself" (Luke 24:27).

We also mentioned the story told by Charles Spurgeon about an aged pastor who claimed that every text in the Bible has a God-designed path that leads to Christ, but that he was prepared, if need be, to "go over hedge and ditch" to find his way to Christ. This raised the concern about forcing an unnatural interpretation of a passage. The best way to avoid this error is to let the Bible show us how to interpret itself, and that means starting with the text's meaning and purpose in its original context. That is the topic of this chapter.

We want to learn a sound method of interpreting God's written Word that honors its origin and its authors (breathed out by God through human authors controlled by his Spirit), its unity (revealing consistent truth and a single redemptive plan), its variety (many books given over many centuries), and its purpose (to lead to God's glory and our salvation).

Our starting point is the observation that the true and living God who speaks in the Bible is the preeminent Communicator. He is so effective in getting his message across to his hearers and readers because he knows his audience as no other speaker could know an audience. When he speaks, he draws on his exhaustive, infinite understanding of our past experience and present situation, our language and culture, our areas of knowledge, of ignorance, and of misunderstanding. Every book of Scripture, from the time of Moses to the completion of the New Testament books, was a flawless "fit" for its location in history and an exact "fit" to its original hearers' needs and capacities. That means that whenever we make the journey from a distant passage of the Bible to Christ, the metropolis of Scripture, we must begin by orienting ourselves to the passage's meaning as God expected its first recipients to receive and understand it.

Our movement toward Christ at Scripture's center must therefore begin with the message and meaning of a passage in its original context—the life experience of its first readers and hearers. We need to understand its unique place in the unfolding of God's redemptive plan through history, based on the revelation that God had already given by that point. How you reach a desired destination depends on understanding your current location, as well as the terrain between where you are and where you want to go. Large shopping malls often aid disoriented

54

customers by posting a map at each entrance with a bright arrow bearing the words "You Are Here," pointing to the location of that doorway. The screen of a GPS (global positioning system) unit helps travelers to get their bearings by showing their present location as well as their desired destination.

Jesus sometimes shows us how important the original context is when he refers to the Old Testament. For example, in Luke 20:37, he says, "But that the dead are raised, even Moses showed, in the passage about the bush, where he calls the Lord the God of Abraham and the God of Isaac and the God of Jacob." Why is the original context important here? Because Abraham, Isaac, and Jacob had already died when God spoke these words to Moses (Ex. 3:6). Jesus bases his argument on that fact. When God says that he "is" the God of people who have already died, this points to the reality of the resurrection and eternal life.

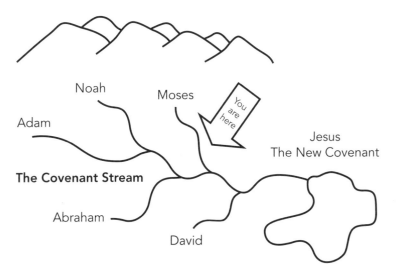

Fig. 3.1. You Are Here

Letting the Bible Interpret the Bible

One of the great commitments of the Protestant Reformation was *sola Scriptura*—that the Scripture alone is the supreme standard and judge for our beliefs about God and our relationship to him, and for our behavior in response to his majesty as Creator and his mercy as Redeemer. That meant that the Scripture itself, as God's own Word, has the authority to teach us how to understand the Scripture. If the Bible itself is the ultimate norm that God has given for our belief and our life, our thinking and our doing, it follows that the Bible itself is the ultimate norm to direct us how to read and understand the Bible.

The Reformers reflected deeply on how the Bible itself teaches us to read God's Word. The times in which they lived required them to spell out what they meant when they affirmed that Scripture is its own interpreter. Opponents of the Reformation who revered church tradition and ecclesiastical hierarchy were charging that when the Reformers insisted on reexamining long-held beliefs and practices through a fresh study of the Scriptures themselves, they were throwing the door wide open to every kind of strange, subjective way to read the Bible. Unless the church and its tradition tell us what the Bible means, said the critics, we will be back in the chaos of the time of Israel's judges, when "everyone did what was right in his own eyes" (Judg. 21:25). At another extreme were those who claimed that the Holy Spirit revealed Scripture's meaning directly to them through mystical experiences, so that they did not need to pay attention to what words or sentences meant to their original audience in their original context. The Reformers had even less confidence in an individual's private experience than they did in a church's long-held and widespread consensus. They were confident that God's voice speaking in his written Word held the remedy to both extremes, so they took pains to clarify the factors that enable us to interpret the Bible as its divine Author intends us to understand it.

One clear, concise, comprehensive summary of what it means to let Scripture show us how to read Scripture is the Second Helvetic Confession of 1566. This expression of biblical conviction was composed by Heinrich Bullinger, a colleague of John Calvin, to express what the Protestant churches of Switzerland believed. In chapter 2, "Of Interpreting the Holy Scriptures; and of Fathers, Councils, and Traditions," these Reformed Christians explained what they meant when they said that Scripture interprets itself:

> We hold that interpretation of the Scripture to be orthodox and genuine which is gleaned from the Scriptures themselves (from the nature of the language in which they were written, likewise according to the circumstances in which they were set down, and expounded in the light of like and unlike passages and of many and clearer passages) and which agrees with the rule of faith and love, and contributes much to the glory of God and man's salvation.[1]

It is amazing that so few words express so fully how the Scriptures interpret themselves. Four factors are identified to help us to discern the true meaning of any biblical passage:

- Language
- Circumstances
- Canonical Contexts ("like and unlike passages," "many and clearer passages")

1. Arthur C. Cochrane, ed., *Reformed Confessions of the 16th Century* (Philadelphia: Westminster, 1966), 226–27.

- Purpose (directing our response of "faith and love," leading to "the glory of God and man's salvation")

(1) *Language.* Because God condescends to speak our human languages, we must pay attention to the meanings and the interrelationships of the words. This means understanding the grammar, syntax, and vocabulary of the languages in which God gave the Scriptures (Hebrew, Aramaic, or Greek). By extension, it also includes recognizing the various literary forms that the first audience would have recognized.

(2) *Circumstances.* Because God addresses us personally in the setting of our experience, we need to notice the circumstances of those to whom the text was first written and spoken: their history, their culture, and their present problems and opportunities.

(3) *Contexts.* Because God's Word is truth (John 17:17), every part of Scripture fits perfectly into a consistent and unified whole, without contradiction or error. So we must interpret each text in the canonical context of the whole system of truth revealed in other Old and New Testament passages. (*Canon* comes from a Greek word meaning "measuring rod" and refers to the entire Bible as the standard for our belief and behavior.) The Second Helvetic Confession implies this canonical context when it mentions "like and unlike passages" and "many and clearer passages." Likewise, WCF 1.9 recommends that when we are wrestling with a difficult passage, we consult "other places [in the Bible] that speak more clearly." This process begins by paying attention to the sentences and paragraphs before and after the passage. Then it widens out to consider teaching elsewhere in that specific book, and finally to any other passage of the Bible related to the text that is our focus.

(4) *Purpose.* Finally, because our God always speaks to

achieve his wise and holy goals, we need to ask what our consideration of a passage's language, circumstances, and canonical contexts tells us about the spiritual need that the passage addresses and the redemptive agenda that God intended to accomplish through it. In general, God's purpose is to evoke faith and love in us, advancing his glory and our salvation. Each passage is aimed toward a specific form of faith-and-love response. So discerning the original audience's circumstances and the spiritual needs that we share with them helps us to discover God's specific purpose for that particular text, both in their lives and in ours.

Let us now survey in more detail what each of these four aspects of Bible study involves, using a well-known New Testament text to illustrate the questions to consider as we explore the language, circumstances, canonical contexts, and purpose of a passage. I hope to show you how each contributes to our understanding of a passage in its original setting, and then opens the way to our hearing its message in the wider horizon of the whole Bible and the whole redemptive plan of God. To conclude this chapter, we will put into practice what we have learned by examining a prophetic message that God spoke through Ezekiel, which combined sobering words to Israel's leaders in their own day with a hopeful promise for the future.

Language of the Original Audience

When we study the Bible, even in a translation in our own language, we need to approach it with careful attention to the language. We want to discover, as well as we can, what idea each word would evoke in the minds of those who first heard or read the biblical text. We want to notice how words are connected to each other in phrases, and phrases linked to each other in clauses, and clauses in sentences, and sentences in paragraphs, and paragraphs in longer discourses such as stories or doctrinal explanations or commands or stanzas in poems. We will ask questions such as these: Which noun or pronoun indicates the agent of the action, and which one indicates the object of the action? What does the choice of one noun in contrast to another reveal about how the author wants us to view that person, place, object, or idea? Do the verbs represent actions that follow each other, or that happen at the same time? Do the conjunctions signal contrasts between ideas, or causation between events, or some other relationship?

For example, consider Paul's well-known summary about God's surprising grace in Ephesians 2:8–10:

> For by grace you have been saved through faith. And this is not your own doing; it is the gift of God, not a result of works, so that no one may boast. For we are his workmanship, created in Christ Jesus for good works, which God prepared beforehand, that we should walk in them.

First, we want to understand what Paul meant by such key terms as *grace*, *saved*, *faith*, and *works*. Within these few sentences, we notice that "by grace" is in contrast to "your own doing" and "a result of works," on the one hand. On the other hand, "grace" is closely related to "the gift of God." Looking at the sentences just before verse 8, we notice that grace is found in the company of God's rich mercy, "the great love with which he loved us," and his kindness (2:4–6). We observe that "you have been saved" is a verb in the passive voice, meaning that "you" are not the agents performing the action but rather the objects of an action performed by someone else. The preceding verses identify the Agent who saves and aspects of the plight from which he saved us: "But *God*, . . . even when we were *dead* in our trespasses, made us alive together with Christ . . . and raised us up with him and seated us with him in the heavenly places" (vv. 4–6). So we move through the passage, noticing how the relationships between other key terms—"through faith" and "not a result of works"—unveil their meaning. A Bible concordance will help us to find other passages in which Paul uses these words, and a Bible dictionary will sum up their significance throughout Scripture.

We also want to see the relationships between ideas in the text, and here is where conjunctions, though so humble, prove invaluable. In the midst of Ephesians 2:9, we read that salvation is God's gift, not the product of our works, "*so that*" no one may boast. The result of the free and gracious rescue performed by God—to which we contributed nothing but our guilt and helplessness—is to squelch in us any inclination to take any credit whatsoever for our salvation. Paul reinforces this point—that God, not we, gets the glory for our salvation—with the conjunction that opens verse 10: "*For* we are his workmanship, created in Christ Jesus for good works." Even the tiny prepositions deserve attention. Since Paul just said that God shows us grace and kindness "*in* Christ Jesus" (v. 7), we want to grasp what he meant when he mentioned that we are "created *in* Christ Jesus." Verse 9 stresses that our salvation was not "*a result of*" our works—not *from* our works. But then we learn in verse 10 that God created us "*for* good works." Our salvation does not result from our obedient actions, but God's saving grace does result in our obedient actions. Of course, even those good works were prepared by God, and so they display his glory.

As we take a step back from the specific words, phrases, clauses, and sentences to see this passage in a larger perspective, we realize that it is part of a letter, written to a first-century congregation. Since it is interpersonal conversation, Paul speaks naturally of "you" and "we." (As we will see below, in Ephesians "you" refers to Gentile Christians from pagan pasts and "we" refers to Jewish believers.) The readers would recognize his use of these pronouns as straightforward, free of symbolism, unlike in Jesus' parables or the visions in the book of Revelation. In this first part of the letter, Paul's verbs present things as they are (the indicative mood, as grammarians would say). Later on (at Eph. 4:1), the "mood" of the verbs will turn "imperative," as specific commands spell out how we should respond to the gospel truth that he told in the first three chapters.

These are at least some of the issues and questions that emerge from the language of a biblical text, and that help us to get acquainted with the meaning that its first recipients would have taken away when they heard it read.

Circumstances of the Original Audience

Because we use language in the context of our personal experience and social relationships, in many respects the meaning of words and sentences varies, depending on who says them to whom, as well as when and where. For example, in our home, as we each read on a quiet evening, my wife might say, "Would you like a cup of coffee?" and I might reply in the affirmative. Now, at this point the words themselves don't reveal whether she has asked out of idle curiosity about my desires, or maybe she is offering to fix me a cup of coffee. (She is kind like that, after all.) But because of our circumstances—how long we have known each other, how much we love each other, the patterns of interaction that we have developed over the years—we can "read between the lines" in everyday conversation. I am not at all surprised if she then says, "Will you make me one, too?" We know each other so well that we both know where this little script leads: she has given me the opportunity to show that I love her!

The living God who speaks in the Bible knows the circumstances of his audience and speaks in ways that make sense in their situation. In fact, he not only knows but also controls our circumstances. And his speech not only makes sense in our setting but also meets our needs in that setting. Even his choice of the languages in which he gave us the Bible shows his gracious willingness to meet us where we are. God gave the Old Testament in Hebrew because the Israelites spoke that language. He gave the New Testament in Greek because Greek was widely spoken throughout the Roman Empire.

When we think of the diverse circumstances and cultural settings in which God spoke Scripture, different languages are just the tip of the iceberg. The Old Testament was addressed to Israelites who, on the whole, worked as herdsmen and farmers, so they easily grasped references to agriculture and weather. Many of Jesus' parables likewise drew on the experience of common, rural folk. Paul's letters, on the other hand, were addressed to city dwellers, some of whom were acquainted with Roman law and Greek athletics and most of whom were exposed to idolatry and religious pluralism.

Since God perfectly shapes his words to the needs of his audience, as we try to listen to any Scripture as though we were standing alongside the members of its first audience, we want to ask questions about their background, experience, and situation: When and where did they live? Were they pilgrims in the wilderness, shepherds settled in the promised land, exiles in Babylon, or a tiny pocket of slaves and laborers in a cosmopolitan city such as Corinth? What kind of work did they do?

Were they farmers, craftsmen, shepherds, slaves, or politicians? Were they poor or were they rich? What religions did their neighbors practice?

When we try to understand Ephesians 2:8–10 in the context of the original readers' circumstances, we are helped both by other passages in the epistle and by other books in the New Testament. In the paragraph following our text, Paul addresses his readers as "you Gentiles" and calls attention to their lack of circumcision and previous alienation from God's community and covenant (2:11–12). Acts 19 shows the spiritual darkness that Paul encountered as he brought God's Word to Ephesus. Even Revelation 2, written decades after Paul's letter to the Ephesians, fills out the picture of the doctrinal challenges that confronted the church at Ephesus in the first century.

As we apply to our text our awareness of these circumstances, we recognize the "you" whom Paul addresses as Gentile believers in Jesus, who were once dead in sin (Eph. 2:1) and alienated from Israel (v. 12). But God made them alive and saved them by grace, along with believers of every race and nation (vv. 3–5). In Christ's cross, the ancient dividing wall between Jew and Gentile has been demolished (vv. 13–16). So Paul addresses the circumstances of the Gentile Christians in Ephesus, as he does elsewhere, by emphasizing the abundance of God's grace. He does this in order to protect them from the Judaizers' emphasis on keeping the works of the law as a basis for acceptance by God and as a ground for boasting (see Rom. 3:17–28; Gal. 3:1–18; Phil. 3:3–11). At the same time, he also stresses that God has created them for good works, in order to dispel the illusion that faith in Christ does not change the believer's desires and actions (Eph. 2:2–3, 10). Seeing the circumstances in which a biblical text was given reveals the spiritual purposes for which God gave that passage.

Canonical Contexts

An important part of understanding where you are is knowing how your position relates to other key places. For example, if you are looking at a map in the mall, it is not enough to see the arrow pointing to where you are; you also want to know whether you are in the middle of the mall, at the far end, near the pharmacy that you are looking for, or near the food court. So you glance over the whole map. If you are hiking in the mountains, you need to know where the river is, where the lake is, and where the highest peaks are. (In chapter 5, we will look at prominent landmarks in the Bible's terrain.) If you can't relate your position to the rest of the map, you will still be lost. In a similar way, to understand any Bible passage, you need to see how it relates to the rest of the Scriptures. This is why the previous chapter was so important; you need to get the lay of the land to more fully understand any particular passage.

When the Second Helvetic Confession mentions considering "like and unlike passages" and "many and clearer passages" as we interpret any text of the Bible, it assumes that because all sixty-six books of the Bible were given by God the Holy Spirit, the meaning of each text will be consistent with what the rest of the Bible teaches. For example, not only in Ephesians 2:8–10 but also in other passages, Paul highlights the doctrine of salvation by grace through faith. In fact, it is a key teaching in letters such as Romans and Galatians. He appeals to the example of Abraham, the great father of Israel, whose experience showed that God justifies the ungodly through faith, not works (Rom. 4:1–5).

Yet the Swiss pastors also knew that some biblical texts seem, at first, to contradict each other. This challenges us to ponder how apparently conflicting Scriptures may present varying perspectives on complex realities. For example, James wrote that Abraham was "justified by works" when he offered up Isaac. He adds, "You see that a person is justified by works and not by faith alone" (James 2:21, 24). Can James's statement be reconciled with Paul's in Ephesians 2?

How can two such "unlike passages" as Ephesians 2:8–9 and James 2:24 both be true? Our confidence that God will not contradict himself invites and urges us to seek an answer. When we listen to Paul and James together on the relationship between faith and works, our understanding of both faith (trust) and works (obedient action) is enriched. In Ephesians Paul teaches us to recognize the difference between faithless works (that is, works based on trusting our own merits instead of Christ) that cannot lead to salvation, and faith-fueled works that result from our already being saved. From James we learn to distinguish a false "faith," which spouts the right words but leaves the heart unmoved and behavior unchanged, from the real, living faith that shifts the weight of our trust from ourselves to the all-trustworthy God. Real faith completely reorients our "center of gravity" from the inside out, and this deep reorientation at the core of our identity cannot help but transform our actions. As Paul himself says, faith takes action "through love" (Gal. 5:6).

The study of words can also help us harmonize the teaching of James with the teaching of Paul. The word translated "justified" in James 2:21 and 24 (*dikaioō* in Greek) can have different meanings. Often it means "declared righteous," as in a legal verdict in which a guilty person is forgiven of sin and approved as righteous. This is the legal declaration that Paul has in view in Romans 4:1–5, as he interprets Genesis 15:6, which states that Abraham "believed the LORD, and he counted it to him as righteousness." But *dikaioō* ("justify") can also mean to "show to be righteous." For example, Romans 3:4 speaks of God himself as being "justified" in his words. In this case, the Old Testament text that Paul quotes obviously is not speaking of the forgiveness of sins. Rather, God is "shown to be righteous" because he is faithful to his promises. If we understand the word this way in James 2, it is easy to harmonize with Paul's teaching. James is not saying that Abraham was saved by his works (that is, James is not claiming that God pronounced Abraham to be righteous on the legal basis of the patriarch's actions). Rather, James insists that Abraham was "*shown* to be righteous" by his works, because those works gave evidence that his faith was genuine.

Another significant factor that makes biblical passages "unlike" one another is their location in the various eras of redemptive history. Over the centuries, as God worked out his purpose in the flow of history, God's words became clearer and fuller. God even adapted some of his instructions to the successive historical phases of his plan of salvation. For example, in earlier epochs, he commanded and expected worship through animal sacrifices. The law of God demanded such slaughter and specified how it should be performed in great detail (Leviticus; Heb. 10:8). But now that Christ has offered himself once for all to atone completely for our sins, animal sacrifices need not be offered (Heb. 10:9–14). In fact, they must not be offered in worship or to try to placate the Lord's wrath, lest those slain animals deflect our trust away from Jesus and the complete, eternal purification that his death achieved. So this is one very important question to ask when we consider how a passage we are studying fits into the rest of Scripture: When were the original readers of this text living? How much of God's big plan of redemption had he already revealed when they first heard or read this passage?

So much depends on where an event occurred or when a command was issued in God's redemptive agenda! When God made his covenant with Abraham, he commanded Abraham to circumcise his sons and all males in his household as a sign that they belonged to the people of God (Gen. 17:10). That sign continued under the covenant that God gave Israel at Sinai. But under the new covenant that Jesus inaugurated, Gentiles who submit to the God of Israel by trusting his Son must *not* be compelled to submit to circumcision anymore (Acts 15; Gal. 5:2). Times have changed. In imagery used elsewhere by Paul, "shadows" have been dispelled by the dawning light of the reality, Christ himself (Col. 2:16–17). God is time's Sovereign, so he freely adapts his words to fit the life stage of his children (Gal. 3:23–4:7).

Purpose

Finally, the Swiss pastors confessed that when we rightly use Scripture to interpret Scripture, the result of our study will conform to "the rule of faith and love" and further "the glory of God and man's salvation." In his wisdom, God always speaks purposefully, with specific aims in view. God's purposes are as broad as the confession indicates: every passage in the Bible is designed to move us to trust God, his promises, and his beloved Son. And every passage calls forth from us a response of love for the Lord who loved us so sacrificially, and love for our neighbors for Jesus' sake. When the Holy Spirit uses the Bible to draw us into faith and love, we experience the salvation that only Christ could accomplish, and therefore God receives all the glory for that salvation.

We can see all four of these purposes—faith, love, our salvation, and God's glory—in our sample text, Ephesians 2:8–10:

- "By grace you have been saved" ("man's *salvation*")
- "Through *faith*"
- "It is the gift of God, . . . so that no one may boast [except

in God]. For we are his workmanship" (so in us "the *glory of God*" is displayed)

- "Created . . . for good works . . . , that we should walk in them" (*love*)

These four interrelated purposes of the Bible should function as "guardrails" as we study specific passages, keeping our interpretation from driving off the road and over cliffs. If we understand any biblical text to teach that we somehow earn our salvation, we are steering in a dangerous direction. If I come up with an interpretation that leads me away from trusting in God and toward relying on myself or anything else, I have slipped off the path somewhere and missed the point of the text. If my understanding of a portion of the Bible does not challenge me to grow in love for the Lord and for others, again, I have not yet seen God's purpose for the passage.

These overall purposes of the Bible—to convey salvation by drawing us to faith in Christ and stimulating our love, to the end of God's glory—apply to every passage in the Scriptures. But the purpose of any particular passage is more sharply focused on some specific aspect or aspects of the whole Bible's "big-picture" purpose. Faith sometimes rests (Matt. 11:28–30) and sometimes acts (Heb. 11). Love patiently endures abuse (1 Cor. 13:4, 7), but it also resists wrongdoing (v. 6) and speaks truth (Eph. 4:15).

Some texts expose and rebuke their original readers' (and our) doubts or disobedience, turning hearts to Christ for forgiveness and for the power to break away from sin. Others comfort and strengthen God's people in hard times, leading them then and us now to respond courageously and patiently to those who make our lives miserable, and to meet scary circumstances beyond our control with hope and trust. Whether a particular Scripture calls us to change or to hold fast, God's purpose for every passage of the Bible in our lives is accomplished as that passage leads us first of all to Jesus (as we will see in the following chapters). Then, in our dependence on his grace, the Bible leads us back into the present troubling circumstances, to which we must respond in faith and in love. In the case of Ephesians 2:8–10, we know that the Gentile believers were facing challenges to their faith and needed reassurance that God had saved, forgiven, and welcomed them by sheer grace through faith. God's grace had rescued them from spiritual death, so they could now lead lives befitting their identity as new creations in Christ.

Conclusion

We want to travel across the landscape of the Bible—with all its variety of times and places and people and types of literature—noticing the scenery along the way as we always keep our destination in view. Because Jesus is Scripture's centerpiece and because, as the old preacher in Spurgeon's story rightly said, only reaching him can make our study of the Word worthwhile and spiritually nourishing, we want to tread the paths and lanes and roads that the Spirit of Christ himself embedded in the terrain of his Word until we reach the metropolis, Jesus. As we have seen, this means starting with Scripture's original audiences in their various locations along the route of redemptive history, listening with them to each passage's language and experiencing their circumstances, and then stepping back to listen to the Word that they heard in the wider context of "many and clearer passages," including those given centuries later, and submitting our hearts to the purposes that God's Spirit is pursuing through his Word: responses of faith and love, leading to our salvation and God's glory. Here is where we start our journey through Scripture to Jesus.

Putting It into Practice: Israel's True Shepherd (Ezekiel 34; John 10)

Ezekiel 34 differs from Ephesians 2:8–10 in a host of ways. Ezekiel's original language is Hebrew, not Greek. Its form is prophetic parable, not doctrinal explanation. It was written over five hundred years before Christ was born, not in the decades after his life, death, and resurrection. It was addressed to Jews, not Gentiles. The list could go on. Nevertheless, the interpretive principles that we have discussed—language, circumstances, contexts, and purpose—will open up this sobering yet hope-filled passage to our minds and hearts.

With respect to *language*, we notice the features of *symbolism* and *narrative*. Prophetic revelation often comes in *pictures*, and sometimes in vivid visions bursting with images that show more than mere propositions could say. Ezekiel 34 is not a vision like the prophet's call in the first chapter; but the Lord's metaphor of negligent, exploitative shepherds and suffering sheep dramatizes the unfaithfulness of Israel's leaders. Israel's leaders—preeminently kings—are the shepherds in view, and God's people are a vulnerable flock of sheep. Spiritual, social, and physical dangers confronting God's people are portrayed in "sheep-ish" terms: predatory beasts, proneness to wander, wounds, and muddied watering holes. Each aspect of the drama has its counterpart in the experience of Israel. Moreover, this pastoral picture sets the scene for a *story*. Israel's shepherds have abused the sheep, so the Lord, Israel's true Shepherd, will dismiss them and come in person to rescue, retrieve, and restore his flock. The narrative genre of this passage means that we can pay less attention to grammatical details and focus instead on the flow of the drama: the shepherds' malfeasance (vv. 1–6), the Lord's verdict (vv. 7–10), and the Lord's coming as the Good Shepherd (vv. 11–31).

The *circumstances* of Ezekiel's first audience were dire. They were exiles from Judah living in Babylon, far from their homeland (Ezek. 1:1–3). News had recently reached them that Jerusalem had fallen (33:21–22). Truly, God's flock had been scattered and ravaged by predators. The people themselves were not blameless, since they heard the prophet's words with relish and promptly ignored them (33:23–33). But their leaders bore the brunt of the blame for Judah's exile.

Stepping back to view Ezekiel 34 in wider *contexts*, we see that the first half of this book announces God's judgment on unfaithful Judah and its capital, Jerusalem (Ezek. 1–24). The second half opens with declarations that Judah's pagan neighbors will also face the Lord's justice (chaps. 25–32). The parable of the shepherds and the Shepherd (chap. 34) begins a turn toward a hopeful future for God's suffering flock, which will include regathering in the land, God's gift of a new heart and resurrection life (chaps. 36–37), and a dwelling place of God among his people that transcends human imagination (chaps. 40–48).

Wider biblical contexts enrich our understanding of the shepherding imagery. Jeremiah, another prophet of the exile, also indicted Judah's unfaithful shepherds and declared that they would be replaced when the Lord "will raise up for David a righteous Branch, and he shall reign as king and deal wisely" (Jer. 23:1–8). Both prophets mention David, Israel's greatest king, who tended sheep before he led people (1 Sam. 16:11; 2 Sam. 7:8). The shepherding image is apt because God had embedded in his people's history the figure of a shepherd-king who fulfilled his role as defender of the Lord's flock. Standing behind and over David, of course, is the Lord himself, whom Jacob had called "the Shepherd" (Gen. 49:24; see Pss. 80:1; 95:7) and whom David addressed as "my shepherd" (Ps. 23:1).

Other "like passages" carry the shepherd metaphor forward into later redemptive history, and thus clarify the future that Ezekiel is sketching. Ezekiel's words about the identity of the Shepherd to come may have puzzled his contemporaries. On the one hand, it is clear that he is the Lord himself: "*I* will seek the lost, and *I* will bring back the strayed, and *I* will bind up the injured, and *I* will strengthen the weak, and the fat and the strong *I* will destroy. *I* will feed them in justice" (Ezek. 34:16). On the other hand, the Lord promises, "I will set up over them one shepherd, my servant David, and he shall feed them . . . . And I, the LORD, will be their God, and my servant David shall be prince among them" (vv. 23–24). Will the Good Shepherd be human or divine? David's descendant or the Lord himself? To this point, David's descendants had miserably failed to tend God's flock as they should. Would the Lord, having rescued, retrieved, healed, and reordered his sheep, entrust them again to David's dynasty?

This is one of many tensions in the Old Testament that cry out for a resolution that can be found only in Jesus. He announces, "I am the good shepherd. The good shepherd lays down his life for the sheep" (John 10:11). He contrasts himself to those who came before, robbers intent on killing and hired hands who fled rather than defending the flock, caring nothing for the sheep (vv. 8, 10, 12–13). In Jesus, at last, we meet the Branch from the stump of David's almost-defunct royal house, who cares for his sheep, fights for his sheep, risks—no, *gives*—his life for his sheep, and gathers his sheep from far and near, "so there will be one flock, one shepherd" (v. 16). He is the offspring of David (7:42), but he is also the Lord himself. In fact, when Jesus goes on to elaborate on how he secures his sheep's safety from all predators, he concludes with, "I and the Father are one" (10:27–30). Those words, as his listeners immediately recognize, are his claim to be God himself, a blasphemy worthy of death (vv. 31–33)—unless true, of course. And it is true: Jesus Christ is the son of David and God the Son in one person, the Word who was God made flesh, come to lay down his life for his sheep and take it up again.

Finally, we consider the *purpose* of Ezekiel 34. For the exile generation to whom Ezekiel brought God's word, this passage brought a ray of hope that summoned deepened faith in the Lord and wonder at his grace. The ruin into which their shepherds had led them was not irreversible. Despite their own unbelief and rebellion, their true Shepherd still cared for them and counted them as his own. In fact, he promised to appear in person to regather them from dispersion, protect them from attack, bind up their wounds, redress injustices, and bring them into peaceful, plentiful pasture. For those of us who have seen this promise fulfilled in Christ and his self-sacrifice for his sheep, the text nourishes our faith in and love for our Good Shepherd. Hearing his voice, by his grace we trust and follow him. And those who are called to shepherd his flock embrace with love our tasks of feeding, seeking, gathering, protecting, and disciplining the sheep for whom the Lamb of God shed his precious blood.

Review Questions

1. What is the best way to avoid error in interpreting a biblical passage?
2. What did the Protestant Reformers mean by the phrase *sola Scriptura*?
3. According to the Second Helvetic Confession, to what four features of a biblical text should we give attention in order to "glean from the Scriptures themselves" an

"orthodox and genuine" interpretation of any passage? Briefly describe each factor.

4. Explain briefly how the factors of the original context help us understand Ephesians 2:8–10.

5. What kinds of questions should we ask in order to get as complete a picture as possible of the circumstances in which a text of the Bible was given?

Questions for Reflection

1. In light of Charles Spurgeon's little parable, have you heard or read sermons that seemed to take you "over hedge and ditch" to bring you from a biblical passage to Christ? Can you discern a clearer "route"—actually embedded by God in his works of redemption and revelation—that connects that text to Jesus, just as England's network of roads links every hamlet to London?

2. In the process of interpreting the Bible, what place do the following have?

   (a) The consensus of the church's pastors and theologians over the centuries.

   (b) The Holy Spirit's impressions on the heart and mind of each reader.

   (c) The text's language, historical setting, location in redemptive history, and relationships with other biblical passages.

3. What can you do to resolve apparent conflicts between Bible passages?

4. If we forget that our study of Scripture must align with God's purpose to make a difference in our hearts and lives, how will that distort our understanding of the Word?

Exercises

Choose two of the passages in the list below, and investigate the following: (1) the language, (2) the circumstances, (3) other related passages, and (4) the purpose. Write down what you learn.

You can use tools such as commentaries, dictionaries, a concordance, Bible software (for example, eSword, Logos, or BibleWorks), and reference notes or introductory comments in a study Bible.

- Leviticus 25:8–10 (The Year of Jubilee)
- 1 Samuel 17:38–54 (David and Goliath)
- Psalm 1 (Like a tree by the streams of water)
- Jeremiah 1:4–10 (The call of Jeremiah)
- Romans 1:16–17 (The righteous shall live by faith)

4

READING THE ROAD SIGNS

Types and Their
Fulfillment in Scripture

IN OVERLAND TRAVEL, how you get from where you are to where you want to be depends on several factors: where you are starting from, the terrain that you need to cross (mountains, valleys, meadows, deserts, rivers), and the system of roads that take you to the big city. So we saw that the first step in interpreting the Bible is to pay attention to our point of origin, to the passage's meaning in its original and closest contexts, which include the language and circumstances of the first audience, other related biblical passages, and the purpose of the passage. This is like standing at the map of a shopping mall and noticing its "You Are Here" arrow, or consulting a GPS to get our bearings in a wilderness. We want to discover, as much as we can, what a biblical passage meant to the folks who originally heard it, in their place and time in the history of God's redemptive plan.

As we reflected on Spurgeon's story, however, we agreed that we do not want to travel from the Bible's texts toward Jesus by going "over hedge and ditch," blazing trails and inventing links that display our own ingenuity, instead of using the "road system" that God himself has embedded in his Word. Far-fetched allegorical explanations, in which some spiritual significance is injected into every tiny detail of the narrative, leave us thinking, "Well, what that author or preacher taught might be taught somewhere in the Bible, but I can't see how he got it out of this passage."

We are not persuaded, for example, when Augustine, the great North African pastor-theologian of the early church, observes that the dimensions of Noah's ark—its length six times its breadth from side to side and ten times its thickness—are the same as the dimensions of the human body . . . and then concludes that the ark symbolizes the body of Christ (*City of God*, bk. 15, chap. 26). When he compares the door in the ark's side to the spear wound inflicted on Jesus and tells us that the wood anticipates Christ's cross, we are dubious. When he reasons further that the church is "the body of Christ" and so other details of the ark's blueprint preview aspects of the church, we are even less convinced. Do the three levels inside the ark (Gen. 6:16) really symbolize Noah's three sons, from whom all humanity came after the flood? Or faith, hope, and charity? Or "the three harvests in the gospel, thirtyfold, sixtyfold, an hundredfold"? Or the three states of sexual purity among the church members: marriage in the lowest hold, widowhood on the middle level, and virginity on the top story? Augustine entertains all these suggestions, but does not commit himself to any; and the variety of these speculations makes us suspect that Augustine's meditation has left far behind the meaning that Noah and his sons (or Moses and his readers) were to find in Genesis 6. We wonder: Was the elaborate symbolism that Augustine developed actually a network of "roads" that the

Spirit of God himself placed in Scripture, leading us to Christ and his church? Or has Augustine, whose brilliance and piety we admire, been "climbing hedges and fording ditches"?

We already looked at a crucial first principle, starting with an understanding of the passage in its original context. Now we add a second: we must learn to discern the avenues that God planned and his Holy Spirit embedded in Scripture, to connect events in Israel's history and passages in the Bible to Christ. To find these paths, we need to look for the road signs.

Some routes are quite plainly labeled, like a major interstate highway with mileage markers and illuminated exit signs, or like a crossroad intersection of country lanes where a signpost stands, its arrows pointing in various directions toward different destinations. The routes that lead from many Old Testament passages to Jesus are marked with unmistakable road signs when one or more New Testament texts explicitly interpret an ancient Scripture through quotation, allusion, or commentary. Students of the Bible call these road signs *types*, a term derived from a Greek word that means "pattern." The study of types—Old Testament individuals, events, and institutions that are shown to foreshadow Christ and his mission by the way they are interpreted in the New Testament—is called *typology*, the subject of this chapter.

In passages such as John 3:14–15, Jesus himself has taught us that we can look for these types, these road signs. In that text, he indicates that the serpent that Moses lifted up on the staff in the wilderness pointed to him. We will study this passage more thoroughly later in the chapter.

What Is Biblical Typology?

You might ask how such obvious, unmistakable foreshadowings of the Savior can be identified. Let me, first, describe what biblical types are and, second, show the ways that the New Testament identifies features and figures of the Old Testament as types of Christ. Third, we will observe that the ancient types and Christ, who fulfills them, are linked through a blend of resemblance with contrast.

We will see, fourth, how typology is grounded in the reality that the Creator and Redeemer who *speaks* sovereignly in Scripture also *acts* sovereignly in history. In other words, the typological interpretation of Scripture emerges from Scripture's doctrine of God, the Lord who acts in history, and it finds expression in the Old Testament as well as the New. The plainly labeled road signs are not exceptions to the rule for reading our Bibles. They are simply the most visible expressions of a deeply embedded pattern, the continuous interplay between God's works and words, that permeates the Scriptures. Thus, the road signs of biblical typology sensitize our eyesight so that we can perceive the subtler signals that mark paths leading us to Jesus.

Finally, we will put into practice our growing grasp of the Bible's road signs or types, eavesdropping on Jesus' conversation with a Jewish teacher named Nicodemus, recorded in John 3.

What Is a Type?

The English word *type* comes from the Greek *typos*, which was used to describe a visible mark, impression, pattern, or model. In the New Testament, *typos* refers to the shape of the scars made by the nails in Jesus' hands (John 20:25) and to the heavenly "pattern" that Moses saw on Mount Sinai, the prototype or template that Israel's craftsmen were to follow in constructing the earthly tabernacle (Acts 7:44; Heb. 8:5). We might picture a metal seal pressed into warm wax on an official document, so that the design on the seal is reflected in the wax. More recently, before computers took over most word processing, there were *typewriters*, which had tiny metal letters—*type*—mounted on metal arms, so that when you pressed a key, the arm moved the type at its tip to strike an inked ribbon, imprinting the shape of the letter onto a page. Newspapers and other printers once employed *typesetters* to place metal letters, one by one, into frames. After the assembled letters were inked, a press would imprint their shape on a sheet of paper. What links all these examples of *typos*/type is the resemblance between an original and its copy, between a pattern and its replica.

That resemblance between an earlier exemplar and its later reflection is in view when Paul describes Adam as "a type [*typos*] of the one who was to come" (Rom. 5:14). In following verses, Paul stresses how different Adam's original sin—"one man's trespass," "one trespass," "one man's disobedience"—was from the flawless obedience of Jesus, whom Paul elsewhere calls the "last Adam" and the "second man" (1 Cor. 15:45, 47). Yet underlying the radical difference between Adam's and Christ's decisions lay a profound similarity: Adam and Christ each acted as a covenantal representative on behalf of others, so each man's response to God affected all those whom he represented. Adam made a choice, and many were affected. Because Adam disobeyed, all for whom he acted were constituted sinners, condemned to death. Christ made a choice, and many were affected. Because Christ obeyed, all for whom he acted are constituted righteous, vindicated in life (Rom. 5:15–21). Again and again we will find that the relationship between ancient types/patterns/previews and Christ, the reality whom they foreshadow, is characterized by this blend of resemblance with difference, of similarity with contrast.

Let me draw together what we have seen so far to propose a description of biblical types. Biblical types are previews embedded by God, the Lord of history, into time and space, into the historical experience of his covenant people, in order to show the shape of things to come. In other words, types are historical realities that God purposefully, sovereignly designed to serve as symbols, pointing forward to greater redemptive realities and events in the future. Types may be *individuals* such as Adam or *events* such as Israel's exodus from Egypt and trials in the wilderness. As we will soon see, they may also be *institutions* such as the tabernacle and the temple.

How Can We Recognize Types?

When inspired New Testament authors actually apply *type* (*typos*) terminology to individuals or incidents in the Old Testament, we can journey on the roads that they have marked out with confidence. But frankly, the use of *type/typos* terminology in the New Testament is rare. So if the only road signs to be seen in Scripture were those labeled with *type* terminology, this chapter could end here—and the "road signs" category would not help us very much to journey with Jesus through his Word.

Happily, the Holy Spirit has provided several other signals to mark the route from ancient individuals, events, and institutions to their fulfillment in Jesus, his work, and his people. Among the most obvious are Old Testament passages that New Testament writers explicitly quote and apply to Christ (but without using the term *type*). Sometimes the Old Testament quotation is introduced with a formula such as "this took place to fulfill" (Matt. 1:22; see John 19:24) or "so it is written" (Matt. 2:5). In the early chapters of Matthew's Gospel, these formulas introduce not only promises expressed in words (prophecy) but also promises embodied in historical events. So they introduce the predictive words of the prophet Micah, announcing that Israel's future Ruler would come from Bethlehem (Mic. 5:2, quoted in Matt. 2:6). But they also preface the words of Hosea, "Out of Egypt I called my son" (Hos. 11:1, quoted in Matt. 2:15), which refer to a past event, Israel's exodus from Egypt through Moses.

Among the individuals, institutions, and events that the New Testament identifies as fulfilled in Christ through explicit quotation of Old Testament passages are the creation of Adam (1 Cor. 15:45, quoting Gen. 2:7), the union of Adam and Eve in marriage (Eph. 5:31, quoting Gen. 2:24), the Passover lamb (John 19:36, quoting Ex. 12:46), David's betrayal by a close friend (John 13:18, quoting Ps. 41:9; see Acts 1:20), the groundless hatred of David's enemies (John 15:25, quoting Ps. 35:19), opponents gambling over David's garments (John 19:24, quoting Ps. 22:18), the transmission of proverbial wisdom by Israel's sages (Matt. 13:35, quoting Ps. 78:2), Israel's deafness to the prophets' words (Matt. 13:14–15, quoting Isa. 6:9–10), and the grief of Judah's exile (Matt. 2:18, quoting Jer. 31:15). Even this brief sampling gives us a glimpse of the complex texture of interconnections that link Israel's history to Jesus as the fulfillment of that history.

Even when they don't directly quote and comment on an Old Testament passage about an ancient individual, event, or institution, the New Testament authors signal how such patterns preview Jesus and his saving mission in other ways. For example, New Testament authors evoke their readers' memories of Old Testament passages and ancient historical events through unmistakable allusions, even collecting a cluster of verbal and thematic echoes of earlier texts and redemptive incidents.

John's Gospel is full of signposts that point the way from Old Testament institutions and events to Jesus, by way of clear allusions. Jesus' body was the "temple" that the son of David would rebuild after its destruction (John 2:18–22; 2 Sam. 7:13; cf. Zech. 4:6–14). As Israel was about to observe the Passover, recalling the exodus from slavery and the start of wilderness wanderings, Jesus identified himself as the God-given, heaven-sent bread to which manna pointed (John 6). At the Feast of Booths, commemorating Israel's forty years in the desert, Jesus announced that he was the fulfillment both of the rock that gave living water and of the fiery cloud that gave light to the camp (John 7:38; 8:12; Ex. 13:21–22; 17:1–7). David had gone from tending sheep to shepherding God's people (2 Sam. 7:8), and his royal successors inherited the shepherd's obligations. But they failed miserably (Jer. 23:1–8; Ezek. 34:1–24). Unlike his predecessors—thieves, hired hands, and predatory beasts—Jesus was the Good Shepherd who would protect his sheep at the price of his life (John 10:1–18; see Luke 15:1–7).

How about the great flood? We want to avoid the forced and unnatural conclusions of Augustine based on insignificant details such as the three levels of the ark and its dimensions. Yet we do have New Testament references that make it legitimate to see the great flood in general as a symbol of the second coming of Christ in judgment, and the rescue of Noah and his family as a symbol of spiritual salvation (see Matt. 24:37–38; Luke 17:26–27; 1 Peter 3:20; 2 Peter 2:5).

Events in the life of Abraham (Gen. 12–22) foreshadow the truths of the gospel. The birth of Isaac teaches that God's blessings come as a result of his promises, not our efforts, achievements, or merits (Gal. 4:22–31; Heb. 11:8–12). Just as Abraham trusted God to keep his word and God counted him righteous, despite his sin (Rom. 4:3–5), so also we receive God's grace through faith, not as a result of our labors. When Abraham went to offer Isaac as a sacrifice, believing that God was able to raise him from the dead, his action clearly pictured what God the Father has done with his Son, Jesus, in costly love for us (Heb. 11:17–19). Abraham was prepared to give up his only son of promise in loving loyalty toward God, but the Lord spared Abraham and Isaac that anguish (Gen. 22:10–18). At the cross, God the Father himself went further: he "did not spare his own Son but gave him up for us all," and at that point no one stopped the hand of judgment (Rom. 8:32). In fact, since Isaac belonged to the family line leading to the Messiah, Jesus was the offspring of Isaac, as well as of Abraham (Matt. 1:2). At the same time, the ram that became the substitute for Isaac is also a preview of Jesus, our Substitute who died for our sins (Gen. 22:11–14; 1 Cor. 15:3).

One more example illustrates the pattern interwoven into the fabric of the Old Testament Scriptures, which the New Testament traces for our comfort and instruction. Consider the patriarch Joseph, Jacob's eleventh son. As we read the account of Joseph's life in Genesis 37–50, many details suggest similarities to the ministry of Jesus. Joseph was rejected by his brothers, almost murdered but then handed over to Gentiles, falsely accused, imprisoned, and abused. Then he was exalted to be Egypt's second-in-command, ruling that great kingdom on behalf of its pharaoh. From his high position of authority and power, he saved the lives of the very men who had tried to get rid of him years before. Joseph seems to foreshadow Jesus' rejection and suffering, his resurrection and exaltation to God's right hand, and the salvation that flows from his descent and ascent.

Is Joseph a "type" of Jesus? Well, the New Testament never says point-blank that Joseph was a type of Jesus. But before he became the first recorded Christian martyr, Stephen, a man "full of faith and of the Holy Spirit" (Acts 6:5) and "full of grace and power" (v. 8), eloquently outlined a repeated pattern in the history of Israel. His forceful speech showed that the Israelites, over and over, had rejected and abused leaders whom God raised up to rescue them from slavery and death.

It happened with Joseph and his brothers (7:9–14), with Moses whom God chose to rescue his kinfolk from slavery (vv. 23–29, 35), with the prophets who foretold the coming of "the righteous one" (the Suffering Servant, Isa. 53:11–12), and finally with the Sanhedrin's condemnation of Jesus to be killed by the Roman forces (Acts 7:52). Without using the term *pattern* (*typos*) or using a formula such as "it is written" or "this was to fulfill," Stephen traces the repeating pattern in the fabric of Israel's history—the interplay of the people's rebellion and God's saving grace—leading his hostile hearers and Luke's believing readers (including us) to the rejected and righteous Servant of the Lord, whose wounds heal us. Joseph's experience, like those of Moses and other prophets, traces the pattern that reveals Christ's suffering and subsequent glory.

As we watch the New Testament tracing the threads and designs in the fabric of earlier Scripture, our eyes, too, will be sharpened to see the shape of the Savior throughout the tapestry. The New Testament overflows with echoes of imagery from Israel's history and Israel's Scriptures, showing how glimmers of grace in past events and practices were finally focused to crystal-clarity through the lens of Jesus, and then dawned in spreading luminance in the people whom Christ redeemed. Jesus himself is our temple, the fullest expression of the "God with us" message of the ancient tabernacle and temple. But Christ's saving work means that "God with us" is not suspended when he ascends to heaven. Rather, his indwelling Spirit makes us, his church, a temple that is the residence of God on earth (1 Cor. 3:16–17; 6:19; Eph. 2:20–22; 1 Peter 2:4–5). Likewise, Jesus is our Passover Lamb (1 Cor. 5:7). And through Jesus we, too, offer sacrifices that please the Father, not slain animals but heartfelt praises (Heb. 13:15–16). The echoes and allusions that link the Old Testament to Christ often stand so "thick" and seem so familiar that readers risk driving past these road signs without noticing how richly God has mapped and marked the routes that lead us to his Son. We need to slow down, to savor Scripture's scenery, and to keep alert to the trail markers that the Father has embedded along the way to direct us to his Son.

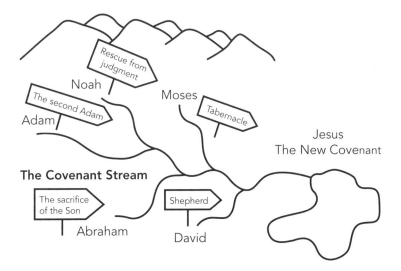

Fig. 4.1. Road Signs

How Do Types Connect to Christ?

As we would expect from some of the uses of *typos* in ancient Greek (the pattern of nails in Jesus' hands) and the analogies already cited (a seal's imprint in wax, typewriters, type for printing presses), one aspect of the relationship between an Old Testament type and its fulfillment in Christ is *similarity* or resemblance. Christ always "fits the shape" of the Old Testament pattern that foreshadowed him in one or more significant ways. Adam made a life-or-death decision that affected many others; so did Christ. In the tabernacle and the temple, God dwelt in the midst of his people Israel; in Jesus' coming to earth, God dwelt in the midst of his people; and by the Spirit's presence, his church is now the sanctuary in which God resides on earth. Aaron and his sons served as priests, offering sacrifice and prayers for others in God's sanctuary; Jesus is the Great High Priest who offered himself once for all to atone for sins and lives forever to pray for his people in heaven itself.

Yet the second feature of the relationship between Old Testament previews and Jesus is *contrast*. The fulfillment in Christ is *unlike* and *better than* the Old Testament event, person, or institution. Jesus brings a deeper, fuller, more lasting blessing. The contrast between the types and their Fulfiller may take several forms.

On the one hand, the contrast may be sharp: whereas his Old Testament counterpart failed miserably, Jesus succeeded gloriously! This is what we saw in Paul's comparison and contrast between Adam and Christ in Romans 5: Adam's one transgression brought condemnation and death to many, but Christ's one act of obedience brought justification and life to many. This diametrical opposition is also in view in Paul's discussion of Adam and Christ in 1 Corinthians 15, especially in verses 21–22: "For as by a man came death, by a man has come also the resurrection of the dead. For as in Adam all die, so also in Christ shall all be made alive."

On the other hand, sometimes the contrast between the type or shadow and Jesus the Fulfiller is a comparative difference between what is *good* and what is *best*. In 1 Corinthians 15, we just heard Paul pit Adam against Christ in sharp opposition: the first man brought *death*, but Christ brings resurrection *life*. But later in the same chapter, Paul paints the difference between Adam and Christ in comparative terms, from good to better/best. Adam's original creation was an anticipation of

Christ's resurrection, which launches the new creation: "Thus it is written, 'The first man Adam became a living being'; the last Adam became a life-giving spirit" (v. 45). For Adam to be created "a living being" was definitely good (Gen. 2:7 precedes the fall into sin). Yet Christ's resurrection as "a life-giving spirit" is so much better!

Similarly, the writer to the Hebrews recognizes that the animal sacrifices offered in the Old Testament sanctuary accomplished a certain type of ceremonial cleansing that qualified people to participate in worship. They produced "the purification of the flesh," although they could not perfect the conscience of the worshiper (Heb. 9:9–10, 13). Christ's once-for-all sacrifice of himself, on the other hand, effects a far better, far deeper cleansing: "how much more will the blood of Christ, who through the eternal Spirit offered himself without blemish to God, purify our conscience from dead works to serve the living God" (v. 14). Animal sacrifices commanded in God's law had a positive role in Israel's worship. But their greater purpose was to foreshadow Jesus' infinitely more costly sacrifice, which achieves infinitely deeper purification.

Typology's Foundation: The Sovereign of History and Speaker of Scripture

By this point, it is obvious that biblical typology would not "work" unless the God who speaks in the Bible were also the Sovereign Lord who controls history. Unless God is able to design real events involving real people in real history according to his plan, when we find striking parallels between earlier Old Testament texts and later New Testament texts, we could attribute the similarities only to sheer coincidence, or to later authors' inventive reinterpretations of older passages and events. If the

Bible were simply a collection of documents produced by finite human beings over many centuries, it would still be interesting, for example, to trace the sacrificial-lamb motif from the Passover in Moses' day, through Isaiah 53, to John the Baptist's declaration that Jesus is the Lamb of God, and then to Peter's description of "the precious blood of Christ, like that of a lamb without blemish or spot" (1 Peter 1:19). But unless the God who spoke through Moses, Isaiah, John, and Peter *actually* spared Israel's firstborn sons (safe behind blood-marked doorways) *in real history* for the purpose of providing a preview of the death that his Son would die centuries later, those intriguing connections would stay at the superficial level of literary influence or the trajectory of tradition. These transgenerational connections would not be woven into the tapestry of Israel's historical experience.

The biblical authors are making a more daring claim. By their typological interpretations of earlier Scriptures and events in redemptive history, they announce that those ancient historical realities were actually orchestrated by God himself to sketch patterns and provide foretastes of his greater agenda, a plan that would reach its climax centuries later in Jesus the Messiah. In other words, the credibility of biblical typology depends on your view of God himself. Because God is sovereign, New Testament authors are not just claiming, "I see an interesting analogy between Israel's exodus and Jesus' setting us free from Satan's dominion. Do you?" Rather, they claim, "God designed and accomplished Israel's exodus to provide a flesh-and-blood preview of the greater rescue that he would achieve at Christ's cross and resurrection." Only if you share the biblical authors' confidence in the living God will the road signs that appear in the writings of the Old Testament prophets and the New Testament apostles set your heart afire.

So types are previews embedded in historical realities and

experiences, and prophecies are previews expressed in words. Both types and prophecies rest on the foundation of trust in and awe before the infinite, personal, all-wise, and almighty Creator-Ruler who is in control of his created universe and of every detail of human history, human life, and human choice. In Isaiah 43–46, the Lord asserts that he alone, in contrast to the dead idols worshiped by pagans, can foretell future events because he alone controls history from start to finish, from first to last. When he speaks prophecy in *words*, he alone can make the words that he has spoken come true. For example, over two hundred years before Cyrus the Great arose to rule Persia, the Lord, through the prophet Isaiah, actually named Cyrus as the monarch who would authorize the rebuilding of the Jerusalem temple (Isa. 45:1ff.). Likewise, when the Lord enacts prophecy in *events*, his sovereign action in past history and future history secures their connection and their certainty. For example, only the Lord could pull off an original creation to forecast a new creation (65:17) or a past exodus to become the prototype for a new one in the future (40:3ff.). Both prophetic words and typological individuals and events rest on the reality that the God who speaks Scripture rules history, and that he is directing every detail of what happens in his universe toward the goal of his redemptive agenda.

Conclusion

The infinite, personal God who speaks in the Bible stands sovereign over every detail of cosmic history—every atom, every force, every event, every person. He has an inconceivably complex and marvelously unified agenda for history: to magnify his own glory by redeeming a people for himself and ultimately renewing his whole created order. As he executes that plan, with increasing clarity he reveals its plotline and central Protagonist, Christ the Redeemer. God has given this revelation both in Scripture's words and in a vast supporting cast of real flesh-and-blood individuals whose experiences and actions Scripture records. As only a supremely sovereign Creator-Redeemer could, the Father of our Lord Jesus Christ has perfectly orchestrated the events of history—from creation, through humanity's fall into sin, to God's promise and fulfillment of the remedy for our sin—in such a way that ancient persons, events, and institutions serve as previews of the redemptive, re-creative mission that Jesus would accomplish in the fullness of time.

Some of those previews and patterns are shown to us overtly by New Testament texts that call them "types" or that affirm that Christ has "fulfilled" ancient Scriptures. Other ancient patterns become visible more subtly as we traverse the distance from Old Testament promise to New Testament fulfillment. Rather than bearing the obvious label "types" or being explicitly identified as "fulfilled" in Christ, these connections often emerge through a combination of verbal allusions and circumstantial parallels. Whether obvious or subtle, biblical types function like street signs to point travelers forward toward the desired destination, to Jesus the Christ.

Of course, none of the previews can match the Protagonist to whom they point. Each is like Christ in some way, so each serves as a faithful template to show the shape of his unique person or his redemptive achievement. Yet each falls short of the perfect Rescuer, Reconciler, Revealer, and Ruler. He alone can repair the damage done by Adam and restore us to communion with our Creator. So whenever and wherever God's Word points out a type of Christ, we ask the Lord to show us both how it resembles the Savior and how he transcends it. Through biblical typology, God kept whetting Israel's appetite for the Messiah to come; and through biblical typology, God prepared experiential and conceptual categories to help both ancient Israelites and us today understand the diverse dimensions of Christ's heroic achievement for his people.

Putting It into Practice: The Serpent in the Desert (Numbers 21:4–9; John 3:14–15)

In conversation with Nicodemus, a representative of the council of Judaism's leaders (John 3:1; 7:50), Jesus suddenly turned the topic from Nicodemus's need of birth from above, by God's Spirit, to his own coming death as fitting the pattern of an incident in Israel's past: "And as Moses lifted up the serpent in the wilderness, so must the Son of Man be lifted up, that whoever believes in him may have eternal life" (3:14–15).

The incident of Moses' bronze serpent, no doubt well known to Nicodemus as "the teacher of Israel," is recorded in Numbers 21:4–9. When the Israelites complained (yet again!) about the Lord's provision of food and water, God judged their toxic unbelief and discontent by sending poisonous serpents into their camp. Many Israelites died of snakebite, moving the survivors to repent and beg for rescue from the serpents' venom. Perhaps surprisingly, the Lord commanded Moses to forge an image of a serpent, the instrument of his holy judgment. The source of venom that reflected sin's lethal power would become the means of the Lord's salvation:

> And the LORD said to Moses, "Make a fiery serpent and set it on a pole, and everyone who is bitten, when he sees it, shall live." So Moses made a bronze serpent and set it on a pole. And if a serpent bit anyone, he would look at the bronze serpent and live. (Num. 21:8–9)

In order to be saved from death, the people had to look at the symbol of the curse they deserved; and they had to believe God's promise that by looking, they would live. In its Old Testament context, to seek life by looking in faith on the emblem of God's judgment was to confront, honestly and humbly, the poisonous consequence of their rebellious discontent. This is not primitive magic, not primitive superstitious homeopathy in which fixation on venomous snakes cures venomous snakebites. Later in Israel's history, in fact, when the bronze serpent cast by Moses was misused as an object of worship, the faithful King Hezekiah smashed it into pieces (2 Kings 18:4).

So there remains something shocking about the Lord's instruction to cast an image of the thing that was causing death and to summon sufferers to look at it in order to escape that death. In the frame of reference of the Israelites' wilderness generation and their children, Moses' readers, the bronze serpent posed a puzzling question: how could a cursed thing set people free from its curse?

The answer to that dilemma would be seen centuries later, when the Son of Man was lifted up on a Roman cross in a form of execution that, as Jews had learned from the ancient Scriptures, emblemized God's curse. To Nicodemus, Jesus simply pointed out the pattern that linked the bronze serpent in Moses' day to his own upcoming "lifting up" on the cross (John 8:28; 12:32–33). The apostle Paul would write that in order to redeem us from the curse that the law pronounces on its violators, "Christ . . . [became] a curse for us," even as Moses had written in Deuteronomy 21:23, "Cursed is everyone who is hanged on a tree" (Gal. 3:10, 13). Between Moses and Paul in God's unfolding revelation, Isaiah described a Suffering Servant who was so wounded and disfigured that others turned away from him, rejecting him as "stricken, smitten by God, and afflicted," although his grief was caused by their iniquities and his wounds brought them healing (Isa. 53:2–6).

In that nighttime conversation, Jesus pointed Nicodemus to a road sign planted centuries earlier in the Sinai desert and the books of Moses, in the historical experience of God's unruly but beloved people. The term *type* does not appear in Jesus' conversation with Nicodemus. Yet the substance of typology—patterns woven into the fabric of Israel's history, drawing Israel's hopes forward toward God's great rescue through the promised Rescuer—is expressed in Jesus' simple analogy: "as Moses lifted up . . . , so must the Son of Man be lifted up" (John 3:14).

When we hear Jesus drawing parallels between ancient events and himself, it's as though we are eavesdropping on those Bible studies with his apostles in the forty days between his resurrection and his ascension. As we hear Christ providing Christ-centered explanations of biblical passages, we can learn how to pick up the clues in our own Bible reading, how to find and follow the paths that will lead us from all sorts of texts to Christ, the destination to which every trail in God's Word eventually leads. Paying attention to the road signs will sharpen our minds' eyesight and sensitize our hearts to discern the complex and coherent pattern of the Bible's single, central story and its Hero, Jesus Christ.

Review Questions

1. What is the problem with the explanations that Augustine gives of the significance of the details of Noah's ark?
2. In biblical interpretation, what is a *type*?
3. Mention the three examples of different categories of types given in the lesson.

4. When a New Testament author interprets an Old Testament individual, event, or institution as a type of Christ, how does this approach differ from what Augustine was doing?

5. What should we learn about biblical typology from Paul's use of *typos* in Romans 5?

6. How can we identify the Old Testament use of typology, even if the term *typos* is not used?

7. List and explain different ways in which New Testament authors identify Old Testament events, individuals, and institutions as types. Give examples.

8. Explain the importance of the fact that typologies show both similarities and differences between the type and Christ.

9. Why is the Lord's complete sovereignty over history absolutely indispensable in order for the Bible's typology to "work"?

10. What does the account of the bronze serpent raised by Moses in the wilderness (Num. 21:4–9) reveal about Christ? How does the analogy that Jesus drew between his own "lifting up" and Moses' action centuries earlier reveal the true significance of that ancient incident in the wilderness?

Questions for Reflection

1. Can you find other features in Israel's ancient history that the prophets saw as foreshadowing coming events?

2. Can you think of other examples of forcing an unnatural reference to Christ into an Old Testament passage, twisting Scripture?

3. How can you be sure that you are not forcing an

unnatural reference to Christ into an Old Testament passage?

Exercises

Can you find any types of Christ in the following passages? If so, explain why you think they are types, and defend your answer biblically.

- Leviticus 25:8–10 (The Year of Jubilee)
- 1 Samuel 17:38–54 (David and Goliath)
- Psalm 1 (Like a tree by the streams of water)
- Jeremiah 1:4–10 (The call of Jeremiah)
- Romans 1:16–17 (The righteous shall live by faith) (Consider the Old Testament context of Habakkuk 1:12–2:4, and the Old Testament example of the "righteous-by-faith" Abraham, Romans 4:1–13.)

5

RECOGNIZING THE LANDMARKS

The Offices of Prophet, Priest, and King

FINALLY, FINDING OUR way from some biblical passages to Christ, "the metropolis," is akin to travelers' experience when recognizable *landmarks* keep them oriented in the right direction as they progress toward their destination. A landmark might be a mountain visible for miles from the plain below. It could be a waterfall, gushing over a lofty precipice into a pool on the valley floor. Or it might be a majestic man-made edifice that dominates a city skyline. Landmarks such as these might not offer the specific directions that road signs provide. But they help us to get our bearings, even if we are not skilled trackers attuned to subtle signals that suggest the lay of the land.

Landmarks: Between the Precision of Road Signs and the General Lay of the Land

As we journey with Jesus through the pages of Scripture and the epochs of biblical history, the Spirit of Christ, who foretold and "foreshowed" Christ's sufferings and subsequent glories (1 Peter 1:10–11), guides our pilgrimage in a variety of ways. Some routes, as we have seen, are marked by road signs. These are the Old Testament prophecies and patterns (types) that the New Testament specifically identifies as foreshadowing and finding fulfillment in Christ, his redemptive mission, and his church.

Other indicators of the Bible's geography and topography are less obvious. The covenant stream that gives structure to God's relationship with human beings throughout history enables us to discern the lay of the land that unites Scripture's diverse landscape. Our Creator has interacted with us through covenant from the dawn of creation and our fall into sin (Hos. 6:7), and then throughout the gradual outworking of his plan to restore the broken bond through an offspring of Eve (Gen. 3:15). Some passages focus on the Lord of the covenant, showing his powerful deeds, his faithful promises, and his worthiness to receive our devotion and obedience. Others focus on the servant's responsibility to trust and obey, the blessings promised to the loyal servant, or the dire consequences of rebellion. The Lord's role and the servant's role intersect in the incarnation of God the Son, Jesus Christ, who entered the human family in order to restore and secure the covenant bond between God and us by keeping the commitments of both parties as the just and gracious divine Lord and the loyal and submissive human Servant.

In this chapter, we are going to survey a third category of indicators that show how the Bible's diverse passages lead to Jesus. In terms of clarity, these landmarks fall somewhere between the explicit precision of road signs and the subtle lay of the land. On the one hand, they are not as obvious as the Old Testament realities that the New Testament identifies as *types* (chap. 4). On the other hand, they are not as subtle as the wide landscape of covenant relations (chap. 2). This middle level of links often helps us to discern, even in Old Testament texts not explicitly mentioned in the New Testament, the route that leads from a particular passage to Christ.

While these landmarks do not provide the explicit direction of road signs, they are easy to see, so they give us a sense of where we are. For example, Pikes Peak dominates the eastern face of the Rockies in Colorado and looms over the city of Colorado Springs, where the prairie meets the mountains. Wherever you are in Colorado Springs or its environs, when you see Pikes Peak, you know that you are looking west and can also estimate where you are in relation to the city's center. Likewise, Mount Kilimanjaro, Africa's tallest mountain (almost six thousand meters, over nineteen thousand feet), towers over the cities of Moshi and Arusha in northern Tanzania. When the cloud cover clears and you glimpse the mountain's snowy cap, wherever you are in or around those towns, you know that you are looking north toward Kenya, just beyond that majestic mountain. Landmarks come in smaller versions, too: the Eiffel Tower in Paris; the Opera House in Sydney; Cristo Redentor with arms extended, overlooking Rio de Janeiro; and the Statue of Liberty in New York City. Each orients travelers to their whereabouts, offering invaluable (though not always precise) direction.

Among the clearest landmarks in Israel's experience are the three categories of leaders that God established to administer his covenant relationship with his people: prophets, priests, and kings. These leaders are sometimes called *theocratic* officers because through them God (*theo-*) ruled (*-cratic*) Israel, the people whom he called by grace to be "my treasured possession among all peoples" (Ex. 19:5), uniquely set apart from other nations.

As Jesus leads our journey through his Word, we can see

that he authorized the use of these landmarks by speaking of himself, directly or indirectly, as Prophet, Priest, and King. He shows that these three roles were always meant to point to him. First, when he began his public ministry, he identified himself as a *prophet* when he read from Isaiah in the synagogue and boldly claimed that the passage was fulfilled in him:

"The Spirit of the Lord is upon me,
    because he has anointed me
    to proclaim good news to the poor.
He has sent me to proclaim liberty to the captives
    and recovering of sight to the blind,
    to set at liberty those who are oppressed,
to proclaim the year of the Lord's favor."

And he rolled up the scroll and gave it back to the attendant and sat down. And the eyes of all in the synagogue were fixed on him. And he began to say to them, "Today this Scripture has been fulfilled in your hearing." (Luke 4:18–21)

Second, Jesus manifested his *priestly* role when he insisted on maintaining the purity of the temple and claimed that his own body was the real temple (John 2:13–22). Finally, he identified himself as the true *King* when he said that his miracles were evidence that the kingdom of God had come (Matt. 12:28). His preaching is summarized in terms of the kingdom of God (9:35). He approved his disciples' confession that he was the Messiah (16:16–20), and he accepted petition and praise as the promised royal "Son of David" (20:30; 21:3–9). The apostles and other New Testament authors followed Jesus' lead, announcing that he is the final Prophet (Acts 3:22–26), Great High Priest (Heb. 4:14), and King of kings (Rev. 19; see Acts 2:29–36).

Buffers and Bridges

Prophets, priests, and kings stood between the Lord and his people as covenant mediators, functioning both as buffers and as bridges. They were needed as buffers because God is holy and pure clear through, a "consuming fire" (Deut. 4:24) whose purity is dangerous to defiled and sinful people. At Mount Sinai, the Israelites rightly realized that having their holy Lord speak directly to them would destroy them. They needed insulation, as it were, from the Lord's consuming glory, so they pleaded with Moses to stand between them and God's dangerous purity:

> Now therefore why should we die? For this great fire will consume us. If we hear the voice of the LORD our God any more, we shall die. For who is there of all flesh, that has heard the voice of the living God speaking out of the midst of fire as we have, and has still lived? Go near and hear all that the LORD our God will say, and speak to us all that the LORD our God will speak to you, and we will hear and do it. (Deut. 5:25–27; see Ex. 19:21–24)

Likewise, Israel's priests served in God's sanctuary, offering sacrifices and incense on behalf of the other tribes. Among the clans of the tribe of Levi, Moses, Aaron, and Aaron's sons (priests) were to camp before the entryway to the tent of meeting, "guarding the sanctuary itself, to protect the people of Israel. And any outsider who came near was to be put to death" (Num. 3:38). Without the insulation of priestly intercessors, even the prophet Isaiah despaired of life when granted a vision of the Lord, "high and lifted up," in the temple (Isa. 6:1–4).

On the other hand, Israel's prophets, priests, and kings also functioned as bridges. Because God is gracious, he intends to restore and retain his bond of love and loyalty even with defiled and defiant people; so he comes to us, speaks with us, reconciles us, rules and defends us, and directs us into paths that please him. Since his personal presence is unbearably pure, he sent prophets to bring his Word. He consecrated priests to approach him with prayer and atoning blood. He anointed kings to execute wise justice among his quibbling people and to wage war against their foes. Through these intermediaries, therefore, the Lord kept his people at arm's length, lest his holiness incinerate them; but he extended his hand to them in words, in atoning mercy, and in strong defense and just governance.

Each of Israel's three theocratic offices operated in a sphere of authority and responsibility distinct from the other offices. Deuteronomy shows the source of this threefold subdivision of the leadership in Israel. As Moses looked ahead to Israel's life in the Lord's land, he gave directions pertaining to kings (Deut. 17:14–20), to priests (18:1–8), and to prophets (vv. 9–22). Kings would wield judicial and military power, so they must saturate their minds and hearts with the law of the Lord. Priests, who attend the Lord's sanctuary, must "stand and minister in the name of the LORD" (v. 5). God's own people must not pursue pagan divination strategies. Rather, prophets who speak truth in the Lord's name must be the Israelites' avenue of access into the purposes of their living God (vv. 9–19).

In Moses himself we see the combination of all three varieties of authority. He was clearly a giant among the Old Testament prophets, receiving the law from the Lord on the mountain and delivering it to the people at its foot. In Numbers 12:6–8, the Lord placed Moses in a class by himself: although the Lord would reveal himself in vision or riddle to other prophets, to Moses the Lord spoke clearly and "mouth to mouth." Moses also had a kingly role both as a warrior and as a judge. Although

Moses' brother Aaron would head the hereditary priestly family, Moses also offered sacrifices to "cut" the covenant (Ex. 24) and to consecrate both the tabernacle (Ex. 40) and Aaron and his sons to their office (Lev. 8). In the generations after Moses, the tasks of hearing and speaking God's word, executing God's rule, and serving in God's presence were distributed to different groups of officers—prophets, kings, and priests. Yet God planned that those three spheres of mediation would eventually converge in one person, the "one mediator between God and men, the man Christ Jesus" (1 Tim. 2:5).

Jesus the Final Prophet, Perfect Priest, and King of Kings

One New Testament passage, the prologue to the epistle to the Hebrews, brings together all three of Jesus' mediatorial roles:

> Long ago, at many times and in many ways, God spoke to our fathers by the prophets, but in these last days he has spoken to us by his Son, whom he appointed the heir of all things, through whom also he created the world. He is the radiance of the glory of God and the exact imprint of his nature, and he upholds the universe by the word of his power. After making purification for sins, he sat down at the right hand of the Majesty on high, having become as much superior to angels as the name he has inherited is more excellent than theirs. (Heb. 1:1–4)

This glorious preamble teaches that Jesus is both God and man. As God, the Son is "the radiance of the glory of God and the exact imprint of his nature." He is the One through whom the Father "created the world" and the One who still "upholds the universe by the word of his power." The Son's divine identity uniquely qualifies him to impart revelation from the Father, and this *prophetic* motif is where the prologue opens: "Long ago . . . God spoke . . . by the prophets, but in these last days he has spoken to us by his Son." God's "last days" speaking through his Son stands in continuity with his speech in times past through prophets, so Hebrews often quotes Israel's ancient Scriptures as addressed to Christians today (3:7, 13). But the superiority of the Son shows that the revelation he imparts is fuller than God's speech in times past, and final.

The theme of God's speaking pervades Hebrews (2:1–4; 3:1, 7–19; 4:1–13; 12:18–29; 13:7–8, 22). Moses was a faithful servant in God's house, but Christ was a faithful Son over God's house (Heb. 3:2–6, alluding to Num. 12:7). Hebrews 3–4 looks back through Psalm 95 to Israel's wilderness wanderings after the exodus. Hebrews draws a sobering lesson from the wilderness generation's unbelief, warning new covenant believers: "Today if *you* hear God's voice, do not harden *your* hearts as in the day that Israel put God to the test at Massah and Meribah." Hebrews 12:18–29 reminds us that whereas God spoke on earth to Moses, God's voice now addresses us from heaven, where Jesus stands as Mediator of a new covenant. The prophetic office has reached its divinely designed destination and fullness in the Lord Jesus, who declared to us "such a great salvation" (2:3–4).

The title "Son" refers not only to Christ's divine nature but also to his royal calling as the Anointed *King* descended from David. Psalm 2 (quoted in Heb. 1:5) speaks of the Lord's Anointed, the King whom the Lord has installed "on Zion, my holy hill" (Ps. 2:2, 6). In the psalm, the Lord promises to give his Son "the nations [for] your heritage" (vv. 7–8), and Hebrews describes him as the royal "heir of all things" (Heb. 1:2). As King, Jesus "sat down at the right hand of the Majesty on high."

This is the first of many references to Psalm 110 in the epistle (1:3, 13; 5:6; 6:20; 7:3, 11–28; 8:1; 10:12; 12:2). In the psalm, the Lord invites David's Lord to take his throne at the right hand, and appoints him "a priest forever after the order of Melchizedek." Melchizedek was a contemporary of Abraham, an ancient monarch who held both kingly and priestly offices (Gen. 14:18; Heb. 6:20; 7:1). Hebrews also ascribes both royal dominion and military prowess to Jesus as the messianic King (Heb. 2:5–9, 14–15; 3:3–5; 7:1–3, 14).

The motif of Jesus' *priestly* ministry comes as the climax of the description of God's Son, in the words "after making purification for sins, he sat down at the right hand of the Majesty on high" (Heb. 1:3). The largest proportion of this epistle is devoted to the themes of Jesus' high-priestly qualifications, his once-for-all atoning sacrifice of himself, and his ongoing intercession as the ever-living Priest in the order of Melchizedek (2:17–18; 3:1; 4:14–16; 5:1–10; 7:1–28; 8:1–6; 9:1–28; 10:1–22; cf. 12:28–29; 13:10–16).

In fact, the overarching theme of the entire letter is probably in view when we read in Hebrews 8:1–6 that "the point in what we are saying" is that we have a High Priest who lives forever to serve in God's heavenly sanctuary. When the prologue speaks of Christ's sitting at God's right hand, this enthronement certainly has royal overtones, as we just noted. But Hebrews also shows that the King in view in Psalm 110 is, like the ancient Melchizedek, also a Priest (Heb. 7:1–28). The location of the Son's throne at God's right hand shows that the sanctuary in which he serves as Priest is not an earthly copy but the heavenly original (8:4–6; 9:11–12). His seated posture implies that his work of atoning sacrifice has been accomplished, completed once for all (10:11–12). Thus, the psalm forecasts the reunion and confluence of priestly and kingly offices in the ministry of Christ.

In these four verses and in the letter that flows from them, therefore, we can see the biblical basis for summing up Christ's mission using the categories of prophet, priest, and king. Now, we are not the first ones to approach the Savior's redemptive mission through these three perspectives. This threefold way of looking at Jesus' mission was beautifully articulated by the Protestant Reformers and the generations who followed them. From the 1560s comes the Heidelberg Catechism, primarily authored by Zacharias Ursinus and received by denominations with Reformed roots on the continent of Europe as a faithful summary of the Bible's central truths. In response to question 31 (Lord's Day 12), which asks why Jesus is called "Christ," which means "anointed," the catechism answers:

> Because he has been ordained by God the Father and has been anointed with the Holy Spirit to be *our chief prophet and teacher* who perfectly reveals to us the secret counsel and will of God for our deliverance; *our only high priest* who has set us free by the one sacrifice of his body, and who continually pleads our cause with the Father; and *our eternal king* who governs us by his Word and Spirit, and who guards us and keeps us in the freedom he has won for us. (Emphasis added)

Eighty years later, an assembly of pastors and theologians gathered at Westminster Abbey in London to reform the worship, instruction, and government of the churches in England, Scotland, and Wales. The Westminster Assembly produced, among other influential documents, two catechisms, larger and shorter, for the instruction of children and adults in the central truths of God's Word. Again the threefold tasks of prophets, priests, and kings were seen as a comprehensive (and biblically grounded!) template to express the various dimensions of

Christ's redemptive work. Answer 23 of the Shorter Catechism (WSC) teaches: "Christ, as our redeemer, executeth the offices of a prophet, of a priest, and of a king, both in his estate of humiliation and exaltation." It goes on to explain the distinctive tasks of each office:

> WSC 24: Christ executeth the office of a *prophet*, in revealing to us, by his word and Spirit, the will of God for our salvation.

> WSC 25: Christ executeth the office of a *priest*, in his once offering up of himself a sacrifice to satisfy divine justice, and reconcile us to God; and in making continual intercession for us.

> WSC 26: Christ executeth the office of a *king*, in subduing us to himself, in ruling and defending us, and in restraining and conquering all his and our enemies. (Emphases added)

These concise summaries capture the distinctive focus of each theocratic office and point us toward how each office finds its final expression in Christ's ministries of revelation, reconciliation, and rule. But each office entails a rich and complex combination of privileges, responsibilities, and related themes. Therefore, a survey of the wider themes clustered around the work of prophets, priests, and kings will sharpen our eyesight to spot these central missions of Christ our Mediator as we journey through the Bible.

The Prophets' Mission and Message

Prophets were agents of revelation and communication. Their *mission* was first to *see* God's glory and *hear* his voice, and then to *speak* his words and *show* his power to save and judge. True prophets were often summoned into God's heavenly royal throne room by means of visionary experiences, to receive their messages from the divine King of kings (Isa. 6; Ezek. 1; Rev. 1:10–20; 4:1–6). False prophets, by contrast, had not "stood in the council of the Lord to see and to hear his word" (Jer. 23:18). On Mount Sinai the Lord spoke to Moses "mouth to mouth," and Moses beheld the form of the Lord (Num. 12:8).

With respect to prophetic "seeing and hearing," the New Testament guides us from Sinai to Jesus along three trails. One leads from Moses to Christ as the consummate Prophet. The second connects the radiance of the Lord's glory to Christ the divine Son. The third relates Moses to us—those who now behold the Son's glory by faith and bring his words to others. First, Jesus is the messenger from the Father who is like, but greater than, Moses (Deut. 18:15; Luke 9:35; Acts 3:20–24). Second, the glory that Moses beheld on Sinai was the radiance of Jesus the Son himself, "full of grace and truth" (John 1:14–18; see also the comment on Isa. 6:1–10 in John 12:37–41). Third, because new covenant believers now behold Christ's glory by faith as we hear his Word, we, like Moses, are being transformed to reflect and resemble the Lord's glory (2 Cor. 3:12–18).

As prophets *spoke* God's words, their message was reinforced by miraculous signs that *showed* his power to save and judge. Moses' prophetic authority was demonstrated by the ten plagues on Egypt, the parting of the Red Sea, the provision of food and water in the wilderness, and other miracles. Through the prophets Elijah and Elisha, God raised the dead to life (1 Kings 17; 2 Kings 4).

God certified Christ's words through his healings and other miracles (Luke 7:22; 24:19; Acts 2:22), and ultimately through Jesus' resurrection from the dead (Acts 2:32–36). As signs, they not only certified Christ's office as spokesman for his heavenly Father (John 5:36; 20:30–31), but also illustrated the message of the words he spoke (John 6:26–51). The signs that the apostles performed in Jesus' name demonstrated that they, too, bore the very words of God (Acts 2:43; 4:30; 5:12; 2 Cor. 12:12).

The prophets' *message* blended prosecution and promise. The Lord sent them to his wayward people to press his legal case against their treachery and treason (Mic. 6:2), to call them to repentance and reclaim their allegiance. Israel and Judah consistently spurned his prophetic messengers, until exile from his land became inevitable (2 Chron. 36:15–16). Yet even in that pit of human rebellion and divine judgment, God remembered his loyal mercy and promised future rescue and restoration (Isa. 40:1–11). So the prophets' task included both demolition and construction, as God's call to Jeremiah showed (Jer. 1:9–10).

Jesus came as the climax to the succession of prophetic spokesmen whom God had sent over the generations, to exercise his divine rights as covenant Lord (Mark 12:1–12). Not surprisingly, Jesus' message, like that of his predecessors, met violent resistance (Acts 7:51–53). So he suffered not only as the atoning Priest, but also as the truth-telling Prophet (Isa. 50:4–7). Yet he also brought God's Word of promised deliverance. When the prophet John waited for God to use his righteous axe to hew down every ungodly tree in Israel (Luke 3:7–9), Jesus pointed John to prophetic signs of healing and hope, not avenging justice, as the signs of God's kingdom come (7:18–23; see Isa. 35:5–6; 61:1–2).

The Priests' Ministry of Divine Presence, Purity, and Peace

The Reformed catechisms focus on Christ's priestly mission of atoning for our sin through his death and interceding on our behalf, but the tasks of Israel's priests were broader than sacrifice and prayer. Clustered around the office of the priests are the themes of God's *presence* in his *sanctuary*; the *purity* and *separation* from defilement that God's holy presence demanded of his people; and the *peace* with God that was restored through *sacrifice*.

God's *presence* set Israel apart from all other nations. Because God in his holiness and grace chose to draw near his sinful people, to dwell among them, the *sanctuary* (first a tent, then a temple) was central to the priests' ministry. Whenever and wherever God came close to his human servants, his divine presence produced "holy ground" (Ex. 3:1–6; see also Gen. 28:10–17). But in a distinctive, long-lasting way, his glory filled first the tent in the desert and then the temple in Jerusalem (Ex. 40:34–35; 1 Kings 8:10–11), setting these structures apart as the places where he met in person with the consecrated representatives of his people. Israel's priests not only served in the sanctuary but also guarded access to it (Num. 1:53; 3:21–39).

The New Testament shows that the Old Testament sanctuaries (tabernacle and temple) have found fulfillment through Jesus in four distinct but interrelated ways: First, Jesus is the true sanctuary in which God dwells with humanity, "God with us" in human flesh (John 1:1–18; 2:19–21). Second, at his ascension Jesus entered the heavenly sanctuary on our behalf (Heb. 8:1–5; 9:11–14, 26–28). Third, Jesus now brings us into that heavenly sanctuary through his sacrifice, by our faith (Heb. 4:14–16; 10:19–22). Finally, Jesus is building us together into a new sanctuary (Eph. 2:21–22; 1 Peter 2:4–5; Rev. 21:2, 9–26).

Because the priests were the custodians of God's holy dwelling, they were also the guardians of its *purity*, enforcing *separation* from all that would bring defilement. The inviolable holiness of the Lord who drew near to Israel dictated standards of purity that emanated from the sanctuary to set Israel apart from its pagan neighbors in diet and dress, in calendar and conduct. God's holy people were to avoid nonkosher meats (Lev. 11). The Israelites' separation was expressed in how they farmed and what they wore, as well as the food on their tables (Deut. 22:9–11). They were to observe the Sabbath, annual festivals, sabbatical years, and the Jubilee year (Ex. 20:8–11; 23:10–17; Lev. 25:8–22). Defects and discharges of the body rendered persons "unclean," excluded from the holy assembly (Lev. 12–15). Priests were to be the propagators and enforcers of this life-pervading purity, so their failures infected the entire nation (Mal. 1:6–2:9). Only God's promises to purge the priesthood gave God's stained people hope (Zech. 3; Mal. 3:1–4).

Christ fulfilled the priests' calling to purity in unexpected and marvelous ways. He himself was "holy, innocent, unstained, separated from sinners" (Heb. 7:26–27), yet he associated with polluted people (Matt. 9:10–11). His fulfillment of dietary regulations (and, with them, rules about fabric and farming) rendered them obsolete (Mark 7:14–19; Acts 10:15, 28). Yet under his new covenant, those whom he has made priests to God still eat every bite to the glory of God (1 Cor. 10:31). His touch cleansed lepers (Matt. 8:3), and his grace welcomed outcasts (Acts 8:26–38; see Isa. 56:3–8). He filled Israel's ancient feasts with significance (John 6:4, 51; 7:2, 37–39).

Israel's priests offered *sacrifices* as means by which worshipers could receive and enjoy God's *peace*. In atonement sacrifices (sin offerings, climaxing on the annual Day of Atonement), a substitute's blood was shed, removing guilt and liability to lethal curse from worshipers (Lev. 4–7; 16). Fellowship sacrifices celebrated the restoration of communion between the Lord and his people, as portions were consumed on the altar but the remainder was consumed by priests and worshipers together

(Lev. 3; 7:11–18; Deut. 14:22–26). In consecration offerings, of animals or grains, worshipers presented their first and best in gratitude to the God who owns and gives everything (Ex. 22:29–30; Lev. 2).

The New Testament shows Jesus as fulfilling the atonement sacrifices through consecrating himself (John 17:19) and offering himself on the cross (Rom. 5:9–10; Eph. 1:7). He is the Suffering Servant whose shed blood fulfills both the Passover lamb and the Day of Atonement victim (John 1:29; 1 Cor. 5:7; Heb. 9:13–14; 1 Peter 1:18–19; 2:24; Rev. 7:14; see Isa. 53:4–9). There is no more need for blood to be shed to avert the curse that sin deserves (Heb. 10:12–18). Yet Christians still offer sacrifices that celebrate peace with God and express the devotion that his grace evokes in grateful hearts. We offer our bodies as living sacrifices (Rom. 12:1) and spiritual sacrifices (1 Peter 2:5) that include words of praise to God and deeds of compassion toward others (Heb. 13:15–16).

The Kings' Righteous Warfare and Wise Rule

Israel's kings were mediators of God's *rule* over his people. Through them, the Lord provided rescue and protection, leadership, and justice. The Israelites' demand that Samuel give them a king "like other nations" was wrong, but their grasp of the king's mission was right: "that our king may judge us and go out before us and fight our battles" (1 Sam. 8:20). The king fights for God's people with courageous faith, leads them with accountable authority, and judges them in wise justice. These themes are found together in the image of the shepherd, which often in the Old Testament pictures the kings' role and responsibility. David, who became the standard for Israel's kings (1 Kings 11:4; 15:3; etc.), had shepherded sheep before his anointing (1 Sam. 16:11;

17:34–36). In Ezekiel 34, the Lord rebukes shepherds who had failed miserably to fulfill the kings' duties: finding and gathering scattered sheep (vv. 11–12), leading them to pastureland (vv. 13–14), rescuing them from predators (v. 8), strengthening the weak and bandaging the wounded (v. 16), and disciplining the strong who bullied the defenseless (vv. 17–19).

Jesus' title *Christ* ("Anointed One," corresponding to the Hebrew *Mashiach*, reflected in English as *Messiah*) refers preeminently to his kingly office, and to the anointing by God's Spirit that empowered him to defend, lead, and judge his flock (Acts 2:36; 10:38; see 1 Sam. 16:1–13; Ps. 2:7). Jesus is the son of David who, like his ancestor, "comes in the name of the Lord" to wage war against his people's enemies, who are God's enemies (Matt. 21:9; see 1 Sam. 17:45; Ps. 118:10–12, 26). The New Testament sometimes presents Christ's death more as a royal-military victory than as a priestly sacrifice (Col. 2:14–15; Heb. 2:14–15). His shed blood is the weapon by which his followers have conquered their accuser (Rev. 12:11). United to our King by faith and arrayed in his armor, Jesus' followers still wage war against spiritual forces of evil, but with confidence that Christ's victory has already secured ours (Rom. 13:12–14; Eph. 6:10–18; see Isa. 11:1–5; 59:15–19). Our conquering King, the Word of God, who is King of kings, will return in the end to wage war against and destroy all evil (Rev. 19:11–16).

I hope this brief survey of themes associated with each office—prophet, priest, and king—has given you a taste of the pervasiveness of these landmarks throughout the terrain of the Bible. Can you see how they help us trace trails and tributaries that direct us, at last, to our all-sufficient Savior? Passages saturated with *revelation* motifs—seeing and hearing God, speaking and showing his majesty and mercy, his judgment and rescue—flow finally to Jesus, the final Prophet. *Reconciliation* themes—God's presence dwelling with us, demanding purity and producing peace—draw us to Jesus, the Great High Priest. Texts that focus on *rescue* from foes and righteous *rule* relate, finally, to Jesus, the Lord's Anointed, the King of kings.

Conclusion

So now we can add detail to our "map" of the covenantal texture of the Bible by attending to the distinctive ministries assigned to prophets, priests, and kings and by noting how Israel's prophetic, priestly, and royal figures functioned (sometimes well, too often poorly) as intermediaries of the Lord's truth, presence, and rule to and among his people. Their moments of faithfulness in office provided previews of Jesus' ministries as the final Prophet, perfect Priest, and King of kings; and their failures kept believers' hearts looking forward in hope to his eventual arrival.

How does identifying these three offices help us interpret the Old Testament? Let's look at practical ways in which each office can help us.

Prophet

As we read the books of the prophets, with their words of warning and indictment and comfort and hope, we must recognize that wherever and however and through whomever the Word of God comes to us, it is Jesus who is exercising his office of Prophet, "revealing to us, by his word and Spirit, the will of God for our salvation" (WSC 24). Wherever in the Bible we meet themes such as the Word of God, the miracles that verify true prophets, the Spirit's initiative to bring God's Word, and even the general themes of speaking and hearing, there the landmark of Jesus' mission as the Great Prophet

Three Offices

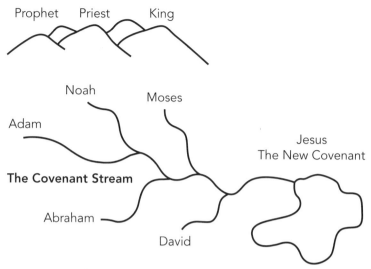

Fig. 5.1. Landmarks

points the way to how those passages connect to Jesus, the Word made flesh.

As we journey with Jesus through the pages of his Word with our eyes alert to the landmark of the prophetic office, we will approach the Bible with questions such as these in mind: Is there a prophet of God in this text, a spokesman who brings—or should bring—God's truth to God's people? Is the prophet faithful to his mission of revelation, or unfaithful, or a mixture of faithfulness and unfaithfulness? How does his faithfulness preview Jesus? How does his failure reveal the need for Jesus, the final Word, to come? Are the prophet's words reinforced by miraculous signs? Do those signs correspond to signs performed by Jesus, the final Word? Does this prophetic word press God's lawsuit against guilty people and predict coming judgment? How do such words accuse us, too, and so turn us to Jesus, who bore our judgment? Does this prophetic word promise God's mercy and relief in the face of present suffering? How is Jesus the full and final "Yes" to all of God's prophetic promises of salvation?

Priest

When we read biblical texts that contain the themes and motifs associated with priestly service and the purification necessary for approach into the presence of God—for the joy of worship before the throne of God—we should be asking these questions: How does this text relate to the priestly service of Jesus, to his supremely worthy sacrifice of himself, to his present priestly intercession for his people, and to his Spirit's relentless labor to purify believers and build us into the new, living temple? How does the wide spectrum of Scripture's priestly passages that touch on themes such as sanctuary, separation, sacrifice, and supplication unveil Jesus' multifaceted ministry as our Great High Priest:

- To cleanse our consciences and free us from the threat of eternal death by offering up himself as our once-for-all, atonement-achieving Substitute and Sacrifice?
- To qualify us to draw near to God in adoring worship and confident prayer?
- To make us his new and living sanctuary, where our corporate unity and purity display his glory?
- To consecrate us to his service even in the nitty-gritty of daily life, where we eat and drink and do all things as holy servants to exhibit God's glory and reflect his love toward others (1 Cor. 8:13; 10:31)?

Paul uses priestly-sacrificial imagery to sum up the appropriate response that we must make to the mercies of God in every aspect of our lives, everywhere and every moment of every day:

"I appeal to you therefore, brothers, by the mercies of God, to present your bodies as a living sacrifice, holy and acceptable to God, which is your spiritual worship" (Rom. 12:1). We offer ourselves in response to Jesus' priestly offering of himself.

King

Kings were anointed to defend, to rule, and to judge. Although the Israelites were wrong to want a king "like all the nations," they understood the king's task rightly: to "judge us and go out before us and fight our battles" (1 Sam. 8:20). At first they had such a champion in Saul (1 Sam. 11). Later, the newly anointed David succeeded him in this role, single-handedly defeating the Philistine Goliath (1 Sam. 16–17). But only Jesus Christ is the Champion who has defeated and disarmed his people's ultimate enemy. He is the offspring of the woman who struck the serpent's head, as his own heel was struck (Gen. 3:15). Yet the Heidelberg Catechism (answer 32) is also right to teach all Christians that spiritual warfare still rages and that we have a royal calling to engage in the conflict. Everyone who trusts Christ confesses:

> By faith I am a member of Christ, and so I share in his anointing. I am anointed to confess his name, to present myself to him as a living sacrifice of thanks, and to strive with a good conscience against sin and the devil in this life, and afterward to reign with Christ over all creation for all eternity.

Wherever in Scripture we glimpse battles or skirmishes in the war between God's king and kingdom, on the one hand, and Satan's domain of darkness, on the other, we are catching sight of landmarks that point the way to Christ, our Warrior-King.

Wisdom and justice are also indispensable to the king's

mission. Jesus is the wise, just, and mighty Ruler par excellence. The close association of Israel's wisdom tradition with Solomon, the preeminent sage, suggests the connection that links Job, Proverbs, Ecclesiastes, and the Song of Songs into God's new-creation project, to renew individuals as kings in the divine image to create a kingdom community characterized by orderly peace with justice and mercy, Christ's church. Ultimately, of course, the destruction of the last enemy and emergence of the peaceable kingdom in its fullness await the return of the King. Yet his kingdom has begun, and the King's transforming grace enables his grateful subjects and assistant rulers to display the King's wisdom and justice even in a decomposing world. Wherever in the Bible we see justice administered and hear words of wisdom, we are encountering landmarks that direct us to Jesus the Judge of all, in whom all the treasures of God's wisdom reside.

Putting It into Practice: God's Despairing Spokesman (1 Kings 19)

The prophet Elijah stands out as a beacon of faithfulness amid the gathering shadows of the spiritual decline of Israel, the northern kingdom. His description of the Lord as "the God of Israel . . . before whom I stand" implies that he had been received into God's presence to see his glory and hear his voice (1 Kings 17:1). He spoke God's Word boldly, and his message was confirmed by miraculous signs of judgment (drought) and salvation (resurrection). We are surprised, therefore, in the aftermath of the Lord's great victory over the 450 prophets of Baal at Mount Carmel, by Elijah's response of fear, discouragement, and complaint toward the Lord.

Baal, the Canaanite storm god, had remained mute and impotent as his worshipers slashed their bodies hour after hour.

When it became Elijah's turn to show what the Lord could do, the prophet's simple prayer brought a blazing bolt of fire from heaven, and a waterlogged sacrifice and altar went up in smoke and steam in an instant. The Israelites responded as they should, exclaiming, "The LORD, he is God; the LORD, he is God" (1 Kings 18:39). The prophets of Baal were slaughtered that very afternoon. And in mercy the Lord relieved the drought that had lasted three and a half years, sending rain in torrents.

But Israel's king, Ahab, reported the events to his pagan queen, Jezebel, and she sent a death threat to Elijah. Unexpectedly, the prophet of the Lord, who had courageously withstood 450 prophets, "was afraid, and he arose and ran for his life" (1 Kings 19:3). Elijah had stood tall and strong for the Lord and his word at Carmel, a fitting preview of the incarnate Word who would stand alone amid a raging mob of vicious enemies, abandoned by his feeble friends. But now the prophet's faith faltered, and he came to the brink of hinting that the Lord who had commissioned him had failed to back him in a crunch.

Elijah had had "enough" (1 Kings 19:4). He was conflicted, wanting the Lord to take his apparently fruitless life (v. 5) but not wanting others to do so. When he reached Mount Horeb, Elijah stated the source of his discouragement twice: "I have been very jealous for the LORD, the God of hosts. For the people of Israel have forsaken your covenant, thrown down your altars, and killed your prophets with the sword, and I, even I only, am left, and they seek my life, to take it away" (vv. 10, 14). He had kept his covenant commitment as the Lord's servant, not only as any Israelite should but also in his special office as God's messenger. He used the title "the God of hosts," appealing to the Lord's role as Protector and Defender of his faithful servant. In the age-old warfare between the serpent and the offspring of the woman (Gen. 3:15), it seemed to Elijah that the woman's offspring had been reduced to a single faithful individual, himself: "I, even I only, am left." When the prophet's foes prevailed, the Lord's cause would be lost.

The Lord corrected his downcast prophet's bleak misperception, expanding his horizon to view the community of the faithful who surrounded him. But the Lord also directed his sight forward in time, to preview those whom God would use in the next generation.

Elijah's experience lies along a prophetic path that leads from Sinai to Calvary, from Moses to Jesus. The echoes of Moses' ministry in this text are many: The angel of the Lord provided bread and water in the wilderness, so that the servant of the Lord could travel forty days and nights (reflecting Israel's forty years). Both prophets stood on Horeb, the Mount of God where both saw the Lord's glory. Both hid their faces as the Lord's glory passed. To both the Lord demonstrated his presence in wind, earthquake, and fire. Yet for Elijah there was a difference: the Lord was not in the wind, earthquake, or fire, but rather in "a low whisper" (1 Kings 19:11–12).

Those terrifying displays of destructive power would have conveyed the presence of the Almighty Creator, who is jealous for his own glory (Ex. 19:16–20). But Elijah needed to hear another side of the God of hosts, a whisper that bordered on silence (see Job 4:16; Ps. 107:29). If he had been expecting either a popular uprising or an immediate divine act to destroy Ahab and Jezebel, the prophet must learn to await God's timing. Can you hear in Elijah's lament an advance echo of the misgivings of John (Luke 7:18–19), the prophet who would come in the spirit and power of Elijah (1:17), announcing the Lord's arrival with unquenchable fire (3:17), when he found himself imprisoned by a corrupt king and his bloodthirsty wife (Matt. 14:1–12)? The Lord assured Elijah that in due time he would bring judgment on the wicked

(1 Kings 19:15–17). For John the Baptist's encouragement, on the other hand, Jesus pointed to displays of grace (healing for the infirm, good news to the poor) that exemplified the quiet way in which he was inaugurating his messianic kingdom.

Unbeknown to Elijah, he was not alone in his zeal for the Lord. The Lord had kept a faithful remnant of seven thousand for himself, even in the apostate northern kingdom (1 Kings 19:18). What Elijah had overlooked in his frustration with God's quiet methods was that Elijah was not, after all, the solitary offspring of the woman who would do battle, one on one, with the serpent. He was zealous for the Lord, to be sure, but he was not the One who could actually say, "Zeal for your house will consume me" (John 2:17, quoting Ps 69:9). The day would come when God's enemies would circle like jackals around the solitary faithful Spokesman of the Lord as he died, alone, on a cross. Jesus is God's gentle whisper, crucified in weakness but raised in power. His voice now addresses us, not on the earthly Sinai but from the heavenly Jerusalem, summoning us to persevering faith to hear and speak his Word, which quietly achieves the purposes for which the Lord sends it (Isa. 55:10–11).

Review Questions

1. What are the three theocratic offices that serve as landmarks to find our way to Christ in the Scriptures? What is the key function of each office?

2. What is it about God's character and our character that requires that we have buffers to insulate us when he comes close, as well as bridges to span the distance between our Creator and us? In what ways did Israel's offices function as buffers and bridges between the Lord and the people?

3. How do the words in the opening of Hebrews (1:1–4) reveal Christ's prophetic role in revealing God's truth? His priestly role in atoning for sin? His kingly role in ruling? Later in Hebrews, where do these themes reappear?

4. How do the Heidelberg and Westminster Shorter Catechisms characterize Jesus' mission as our Redeemer and Mediator?

5. Explain how identifying each of the offices of prophet, priest, and king helps us interpret the Old Testament.

Questions for Reflection

1. How are the roles of prophet, priest, and king manifested in us as people created in the image of God? (See Gen. 1–2; Eph. 4:24; Col. 3:10.)

2. In what ways do you reflect the image of God as prophet, priest, and king in your everyday life?

Exercises

Can you find any landmarks pointing to Christ in the following passages (think of the three offices)? If so, explain what they teach us about Christ.

- Leviticus 25:8–10 (The Year of Jubilee)
- 1 Samuel 17:38–54 (David and Goliath)
- Psalm 1 (Like a tree by the streams of water)
- Jeremiah 1:4–10 (The call of Jeremiah)
- Romans 1:16–17 (The righteous shall live by faith) (With which Old Testament office do themes of righteousness and judgment connect most closely?)

6

"ARE WE THERE YET?"

How Journeying with Jesus through His Word Changes Us

WE HAVE COMPARED reading the Bible to taking a journey. We began with a brief trek from Jerusalem to the village of Emmaus. During that journey, two downcast disciples with dashed hopes became men whose hearts flamed with joy as their mysterious traveling Companion showed them from the Scriptures God's plan to lead his Messiah through suffering into glory and, through that Messiah, to lead others out of spiritual death into eternal life. As they traveled those miles, their conversation traversed millennia: from the garden of God to the still-future new Jerusalem, from Adam and Eve's exile at history's dawn to God's embrace through grace at history's destination.

We have surveyed the ways that God has marked out the paths and avenues that lead through the Bible's various territories and terrains to Jesus, that long-promised Messiah who was showing those two disciples that he and his saving mission are the themes that unify the Law, the Prophets, the Psalms, and other Scriptures. As this book comes to a close, I hope your and my journey with Jesus through his Word will continue for the rest of our days.

What will this Christ-focused way of exploring the Bible do to us and in us? When the two disciples and their unrecognized Teacher reached Emmaus, they offered him hospitality over supper. Surprisingly, he took the host's role, breaking the bread. Suddenly their eyes were opened and they saw Jesus for who he is. Afterward they recalled, "Did not our hearts burn within us while he talked to us on the road, while he opened to us the Scriptures?" (Luke 24:32). Some weeks later, Jesus' followers were no longer hiding in secrecy and cringing in fear but rather announcing, publicly and boldly, the meaning of Jesus' death and the reality of his resurrection. When the authorities "saw the boldness of Peter and John, and perceived that they were uneducated, common men, they were astonished. And they recognized that they had been with Jesus" (Acts 4:13). Can "being with Jesus" still make such a radical change in our lives that others notice the difference? If so, how can we spend such transformative time with this Lord of glory?

On the evening before his crucifixion, Jesus prepared his closest disciples for his imminent departure—not just his death, but his ascent to heaven after his resurrection from the dead. Though he would soon be absent from them physically, he nevertheless promised that he would continue to keep God's "Immanuel" ("God with us") commitment in another way. "I will not leave you as orphans; I will come to you" (John 14:18). How would he come? He had just told them: "I will ask the Father, and he will give you another Helper, to be with you forever, even the Spirit of truth, whom the world cannot receive, because it neither sees him nor knows him. You know him, for he dwells with you and will be in you" (vv. 16–17). Through the personal presence of the Holy Spirit and the abiding of Jesus' words in their hearts, the triune God would continue to be with those who believe in the Son:

> Whoever has my commandments and keeps them, he it is who loves me. And he who loves me will be loved by my Father, and I will love him and manifest myself to him. . . . If anyone loves me, he will keep my word, and my Father will love him, and we will come to him and make our home with him. (John 14:21–23)

Through the Spirit who indwells us and the Word of Jesus that stays with us, God the Father and Jesus the Son take up residence with and in us. Though he has bodily ascended to God's right hand in heaven, the risen Christ is still our traveling Companion on earth, keeping his promise, "I will never leave you nor forsake you" (Heb. 13:5). Because "Jesus Christ is the same yesterday and today and forever" (v. 8), we can and must approach the Bible, whenever we read and study it, expecting that Paul's prayer for the Ephesians will be answered for us as well: that God will "give you [the Spirit] of wisdom and of revelation in the knowledge of him, having the eyes of your hearts enlightened" to "know . . . the hope to which he has called you, . . . the riches of his glorious inheritance in the saints, and . . . the immeasurable greatness of his power toward us who believe, according to the working of his great might that he worked in Christ" (Eph. 1:17–20). As we journey through God's Word in the company of Christ's Spirit, with our minds and hearts attuned to the perspectives that the risen Lord Jesus imparted to his first followers as he led them through the Scriptures, we will find that our living Savior is moving us to marvel and worship, to hope and trust, and to become more like himself.

Journeying with Jesus Moves Us to Marvel and Worship

The interconnections throughout the Bible—a collection of documents written over a millennium and a half, through dozens of authors to audiences in a variety of living situations—should move us to marvel at the wisdom and sovereign power of God. All the characters who populate the drama of the Bible's history of redemption, all the plots and subplots, are bound together into one unified story of conflict and triumph by one Hero, Jesus the Messiah, Son of God and Son of Man.

If we were dealing with a work of fiction composed by a single author in a single generation, we might not be surprised to encounter a consistent and coherent plotline in which every detail finally falls into place at the story's finale. But the Bible's plotline focuses on actual persons and historical events, not the products of a human imagination. To be able to weave so many real people, flaws and all, and their various actions, good and bad, into a single narrative tapestry that reaches its focal point and fulfillment in one Galilean who is Savior of the world, the Author of the story would have to be none other than the Sovereign Planner and Orchestrator of everything that happens everywhere, over the whole span of human history and cosmic time.

This is, in fact, exactly what the Scriptures claim about their divine Author: he has a purpose for everything that he has created (which is everything other than himself, the Creator), and he "works all things according to the counsel of his will"

(Eph. 1:11). At the center of God's invincible agenda for cosmic history is "his purpose, which he set forth in Christ as a plan for the fullness of time, to unite all things in him, things in heaven and things on earth" (vv. 9–10). It is no wonder, then, that we find these words of Paul in the midst of an outpouring of astonished adoration that begins, "Blessed be the God and Father of our Lord Jesus Christ, who has blessed us in Christ with every spiritual blessing in the heavenly places" (v. 3). Later in the letter, Paul marveled over the divine grace that granted to him, "the very least of all the saints," the privilege to preach "the unsearchable riches of Christ, and to bring to light for everyone what is the plan of the mystery hidden for ages in God who created all things, so that through the church the manifold wisdom of God might now be made known . . . according to the eternal purpose that he has realized in Christ Jesus our Lord" (3:8–11). God's one eternal plan, brought to fruition in one person, "Christ Jesus our Lord," displays the splendor of his multifaceted wisdom.

Nebuchadnezzar, a powerful pagan monarch accustomed to getting his own way, endured abject humiliation for his preening arrogance. When he finally came to his senses, he had caught a glimpse of the true Sovereign whose will cannot be thwarted, so he confessed in wonder and in worship:

> I blessed the Most High, and praised and honored him who lives forever,
>
> for his dominion is an everlasting dominion,
>> and his kingdom endures from generation to generation;
> all the inhabitants of the earth are accounted as nothing,
>> and he does according to his will among the host of heaven
>> and among the inhabitants of the earth;

and none can stay his hand
    or say to him, "What have you done?" (Dan. 4:34–35)

You and I have far more reason to marvel and to bow in adoration as we journey, page by page, through God's Word, discovering vista after vista of his power, purity, faithfulness, and mercy. We watch him patiently guide the passing generations and unfolding ages toward the arrival of Jesus, the promised offspring of the woman, descendant of Abraham, final and faithful Israel, perfect Priest and Sacrifice, royal son of David, last and best Word from God the Father. The road signs, landmarks, and lay of the land that reveal the paths that finally converge in Christ are not given merely to intrigue our minds with tantalizing, unexpected connections across the centuries. They move our hearts to marvel over God's manifold wisdom, to adore him for his surprising concern for rebels like us, for his astounding skill in devising the plan for our rescue, and for the astonishing price he paid to execute that plan. Journeying with Jesus through his Word, we find ourselves blending our voices with Paul's outburst of praise:

Oh, the depth of the riches and wisdom and knowledge of God! How unsearchable are his judgments and how inscrutable his ways!

"For who has known the mind of the Lord,
    or who has been his counselor?"
"Or who has given a gift to him
    that he might be repaid?"

For from him and through him and to him are all things. To him be glory forever. Amen. (Rom. 11:33–36)

Journeying with Jesus
Moves Us to Hope and Trust

Writing about the purpose of the Old Testament, the apostle Paul told the Christians in Rome: "For whatever was written in former days was written for our instruction, that through endurance and through the encouragement of the Scriptures we might have hope" (Rom. 15:4). He wrote those words immediately after quoting Psalm 69:9 ("The reproaches of those who reproached you fell on me") as illustrating the commitment of Christ not to please himself but to please his Father and serve our needs (Rom. 15:3). In fact, it is only because those ancient Scriptures, as well as the New Testament books, bear witness to the person and redeeming mission of Jesus the Messiah that they can bring us encouragement and hope.

Apart from the golden thread woven through the tapestry of biblical history, glistening with the glory of Christ, the Scriptures would present only a dark record of dashed and hollow hopes. Repeatedly across the ages, the Bible brings into view individuals who seem heroic at first glance, but in time prove to be disappointments. *Adam and Eve*, created in God's likeness and image, were placed in a lush and fruitful garden on an earth and in a universe that was all "very good." But they believed Satan's lie, disobeyed their good Creator, and brought guilt and death on all their children down through the generations and a curse on the very earth that sustained them. Yet God spoke a word of promise, a shaft of light, into the midnight of their shame: someday a woman's Son would come to shatter the father of lies and his lethal venom, and the Son would win that victory as he himself would be wounded (Gen. 3:15).

As generations passed, *Noah* was named "Rest" by his father in the hope that he, at last, would bring rest and relief from that curse for toiling, weary humanity (Gen. 5:28–29). Noah was "a righteous man, blameless in his generation," and "found favor in the eyes of the LORD" (6:8–9). Trusting God's word, Noah built an ark. His family survived as God's floodwaters washed the earth clean from human pollutants. Yet even Noah subsequently abused the Creator's good gifts from the earth, and in his drunken stupor he was shamed by his own son. Noah was not the son destined to bring relief from the curse.

Abraham left family and homeland, trusting in God's promise. Yet his faith faltered when he feared that powerful pagan rulers would take his life in order to take his beautiful wife. The half-lie that he urged the lovely Sarah to tell could have compromised the purity of the wife and mother through whom God planned to give Abraham countless descendants, bringing blessing to all nations. Yet the promise-keeping God protected Sarah's dignity and Abraham's life, despite the patriarch's flinching, fluctuating faith. Their doubting efforts to "help" God keep his promise by using Sarah's slave Hagar as her reproductive surrogate only bred conflict within the household immediately and for countless generations to come. Though blessing would come to all of earth's peoples through Abraham's family, the man himself disappoints us if we look to him to vanquish evil altogether.

So where shall we look for the offspring of the woman? On whom can our hopes for rescue rest? *Jacob*? The name assigned to him at birth, as he grabbed his twin brother's heel, suggested one who attacks by stealth from behind, so it aptly foreshadowed his sly, cheating character. He would mature into a shrewd trader—a birthright for a bowl of lentil stew—and cunning trickster, deceiving his blind father. *Joseph*? Resented by his brothers, he endured great suffering in patient faith and was finally exalted to power, to become those same brothers' rescuer from death by starvation. But Joseph died outside God's land, clinging to the promise that the Lord would one day bring his kinfolk home. *Moses*? After a privileged upbringing, the adopted grandson of the Egyptian pharaoh got off to a rocky start as his fellow Israelites' rescuer. Taking matters into his own hands, he imagined that a violent murder, committed in secret (as he thought), could start the movement that would set God's people free. But there was a witness, and when Moses' secret emerged, he fled Egypt in fear for his life. Later, when Israel's fiery Lord commissioned and commanded him to return, Moses marshaled every excuse he could come up with to evade the divine call. One moment strong in courageous faith and the next fearful and complaining, one moment meeker than anyone on earth (Num. 12:3) and the next exploding in frustration and arrogant disobedience (20:10–13), Moses was not the one in whom hopes would find fulfillment.

Could *Israel* as a people be the hope of the world? The Israelites' immediate response to the Lord's book of the covenant was just what it should have been: "All that the Lord has spoken we will do, and we will be obedient" (Ex. 24:7). Yet when Moses went back up the mountain to receive the Lord's design for his dwelling place with his people, they turned their backs on him and worshiped a statue of a calf, cast in gold (32:1–10). If hopes were vested in Israel, they would be disappointed not just once but repeatedly over the centuries, as the sad narrative leading from exodus to exile demonstrates.

How about *David*? In his youth, when anointed as king, the man after God's own heart (1 Sam. 13:14) killed the champion of God's enemies with the weapon that he knew to be trustworthy, "the name of the Lord of hosts, the God of the armies of Israel" (17:45). But later, on the throne, David used God's enemies as weapons to eliminate a loyal soldier, Uriah, in a futile attempt to cover up his own immorality. David falls tragically short of the royal benchmark that God announced in David's own final oracle: "When one rules justly over men, ruling in the fear of God, he dawns on them like the morning light" (2 Sam. 23:3–4).

What about *Solomon*, wisest of ancient Israel's sages and sovereigns? Sadly, his wily political alliances, secured by marriages to multiple wives belonging to pagan royalty, stole his heart away from the God who had given Solomon wisdom. He played the fool and served the idols to the point that God announced that he would wrest most of Israel from the hands of the dynasty of David and Solomon (1 Kings 11:9–13). And so it goes, even among the heirs of the beloved David. King Joash started well, under the spiritual mentoring of the faithful priest Jehoiada; but he ended very badly, slaughtering Jehoiada's son for boldly speaking God's prophetic indictment (2 Chron. 24). Hezekiah "did what was right in the eyes of the LORD, according to all that David his father had done" (2 Kings 18:3). But he plundered God's temple to buy off Assyria and foolishly opened his treasuries to envoys from Babylon (18:14–16; 20:12–19). Josiah purged the land of idolatry and restored true worship in the temple. Yet he, too, resisted God's word at one crucial juncture, and so died in battle (2 Chron. 35:20–24). Neither David himself nor any of his royal descendants fit the profile of the utterly righteous Ruler for whom David himself hoped—not until the appearance of that final son of David, the One whom David described mysteriously as "my Lord" (Ps. 110:1; see Matt. 22:41–45).

The pages of the Old Testament teem with historical figures who evoke our admiration, yet not one of them had the integrity, much less the eternity of life, to bear the weight of our hopes for rescue from sin and reconciliation with God.

The same can be said of the prominent individuals in New Testament history—Mary, Peter, James and John, Stephen, Paul, and others.

Only Jesus himself can sustain our hopes and bring us encouragement amid life's disillusionments, discouragements, despair, and even death itself. As we notice the clay feet of even the best of the Bible's merely human heroes, we realize that we cannot fix our gaze on them, but instead must look up to the Redeemer to whom they looked forward in hopeful faith. As those admirable but flawed figures give us glimpses of the faithfulness, compassion, and holiness of Jesus, those glimpses point us to the Messiah himself. As we journey through the Word with Jesus as our Companion and Guide, pointing out the previews of his glorious person and his gracious mission, his Spirit encourages our hearts and fortifies our hope.

Journeying with Jesus Makes Us More like Him

The New Testament authors frankly acknowledge that because Jesus has bodily ascended to God's right hand in heaven, we who trust him now do not see him with our physical eyes. To be sure, Stephen was granted a vision of Jesus standing in heaven (Acts 7:55–56), and his persecutor Saul (Paul) would later behold the blinding splendor of Jesus' glory (9:3–9). But most Christians "walk by faith, not by sight" (2 Cor. 5:6–7). Peter had been among the "eyewitnesses of [Jesus'] majesty" on the mountain of transfiguration (2 Peter 1:16–18); but Peter also stressed that others' faith, apart from sight, was no less effective in uniting them to Jesus the Savior: "Though you have not seen him, you love him. Though you do not now see him, you believe in him and rejoice with joy that is inexpressible and filled with glory" (1 Peter 1:8).

In another sense, however, even though we do not now see Jesus as his apostles did, we do see Jesus. Paul reminded the Gentile Christians of Galatia: "It was before your eyes that Jesus Christ was publicly portrayed as crucified" (Gal. 3:1). That presentation of Jesus "before your eyes" took place not through visions or visual aids, but rather through Paul's preaching: "Did you receive the Spirit by works of the law or by hearing with faith?" (v. 2). The Galatians "saw" Jesus by hearing the message that Paul preached and by believing it.

Paul drew lines of connection and contrast between Moses' privilege of beholding God's glory on Mount Sinai and our privilege of beholding God's glory in the face of Christ (2 Cor. 3:7–18). Moses' face apparently absorbed glorious light from his meeting with the Lord, and then it radiated that light when he descended the mountain to deliver the law (Ex. 34:29–35). That radiance was visible to the Israelites' physical eyes, and so terrifying that Moses covered it with a veil (2 Cor. 3:13). But that glory also faded over time, signifying that the covenant mediated by Moses would eventually give way to a new, better, eternal covenant (vv. 6–11). The law mediated through Moses brought condemnation and death through the violation of its commands, whereas the new covenant brings us righteousness and life through Christ's redeeming work and his Spirit's presence (vv. 7–9). But there is another amazing difference between Moses' ministry and new covenant ministry: Moses *alone* entered God's presence, so Moses' face alone shone with God's glory. Now, through "the light of the gospel of the glory of Christ," proclaimed by apostles and pastors (4:4–5), "*we all*, with unveiled face, beholding the glory of the Lord, are being transformed into the same image from one degree of glory to another. For this comes from the Lord who is the Spirit" (3:18).

Pause a moment to ponder that parallel between Moses, on the one hand, and *every believer in Jesus today*, on the other. Both for Moses and for you, to behold the glory of the Lord is to be transformed to resemble that glory. The glory that "has shone in our hearts to give the light of the knowledge of the glory of God in the face of Jesus Christ" (2 Cor. 4:6) does not diminish over time, as the gleam on Moses' face did. Instead, it increases "from one degree of glory to another" (3:18). Seeing Jesus through the Word makes us more and more like Jesus in love, purity, compassion, faithfulness, kindness, and truth.

Over the centuries, countless people have read the Bible in pursuit of transformation of their desires and character and behavior. Many have focused on the Bible's many commands and prohibitions. What better way to change than to hear God's directions, and then to muster up the willpower to obey what God has said? Paul himself, before Christ's grace conquered and captured him, had practiced this legal way of reading and responding to Scripture: know the rules, keep the rules. Paul had achieved as much as was humanly possible through this approach: "as to righteousness under the law, blameless" (Phil. 3:6). But when the risen Lord Jesus confronted him face to face, Paul discovered that "a righteousness of my own that comes from the law" (v. 9) would never win approval from the holy God. Paul the law-keeping Jew, no less than the most sensual idolater, was "dead in . . . trespasses and sins," deserving God's wrath "like the rest of mankind" (Eph. 2:1–3). His stone-dead heart needed to be raised up to vibrant, gladly obedient life. But God had delivered no law—no set of commands and expectations—to convey such spiritual life (Gal. 3:21).

As ancient prophets had seen and said, only God's Sovereign Spirit could make dead people live again and turn stony hearts tender toward the Lord and his will (Ezek. 36:25–27; 37:8–14;

see Isa. 44:3–5). The new covenant that God promised through the prophet Jeremiah would bring both forgiveness for sins and the inscribing of God's law right into his people's hearts (Jer. 31:31–34). That is exactly what the Holy Spirit now does as he uses God's Word, written and preached, to turn us around and open our eyes to see God's glory in Jesus' face. After describing the anguished frustration of recognizing how right God's law is and finding oneself utterly unable to meet its standard, Paul exulted in the new way of deep transformation opened up by the redemptive work of Jesus, applied by the life-giving power of his Spirit:

> For the law of the Spirit of life has set you free in Christ Jesus from the law of sin and death. For God has done what the law, weakened by the flesh, could not do. By sending his own Son in the likeness of sinful flesh and for sin, he condemned sin in the flesh, in order that the righteous requirement of the law might be fulfilled in us, who walk not according to the flesh but according to the Spirit. (Rom. 8:2–4)

As you read your Bible, then, be on the alert to catch glimpses of Jesus, for as you fix your heart's gaze on him, the Holy Spirit will carry on his mysterious project to make you more like your Savior—a good work that he is committed to "bring . . . to completion at the day of Jesus Christ" (Phil. 1:6). Should you pay attention to the Bible's many commands? Of course you should, since every command shows, somehow or other, what it means to love God above all and your neighbor as yourself (Matt. 22:37–40). In other words, every command casts light on the loving heart and deeds of Jesus, who gladly kept the law's every command out of sheer love for his Father and for us. But the living power to keep God's commands is conveyed by God's

Spirit as he fixes our heart's gaze on the beauty of God's Son. See him, and be transformed!

Conclusion

As our journey with Jesus *together* draws to a close, I hope that you will keep exploring, as I intend to do. As we do, we need to wrestle, over and over, with the question, "What difference does this way of reading the Bible make in our lives?"

God has not spoken in Scripture simply to entertain us with a collection of brain-teasing puzzles: "Can you trace your way through the maze? Connect the dots? Spot tiny clues tucked away in complex illustrations?" He speaks always, everywhere, for the ultimate purpose of calling us to come Home, along the one and only road that leads to the Father: Jesus, "the way, the truth, and the life" (John 14:6). So our study of the Bible through the lens of Christ must do more than leave us intellectually satisfied. This journey must and will make us different persons: humbled in awe, hopeful in adversity, and through it all growing to reflect the beauty, mercy, and holiness of the Christ who loved us and gave himself for us.

Putting It into Practice: Seeing a Star from Afar (Numbers 24:15–19)

Suppose we find ourselves in an unfamiliar place in the Scriptures, something that often happens to us, such as Balaam's prophecy found in Numbers 24. How should we interpret this passage? More specifically, what can we learn about Jesus from it? If we can practice what we have learned together with a passage like this, then we should also be able to do it with less difficult passages. So let's explore this true prophecy, spoken through an unlikely instrument, using the tracking insights that we have gained.

> The oracle of Balaam the son of Beor,
> > the oracle of the man whose eye is opened,
> the oracle of him who hears the words of God,
> > and knows the knowledge of the Most High,
> who sees the vision of the Almighty,
> > falling down with his eyes uncovered:
> I see him, but not now;
> > I behold him, but not near:
> a star shall come out of Jacob,
> > and a scepter shall rise out of Israel;
> it shall crush the forehead of Moab
> > and break down all the sons of Sheth.
> Edom shall be dispossessed;
> > Seir also, his enemies, shall be dispossessed.
> > Israel is doing valiantly.
> And one from Jacob shall exercise dominion
> > and destroy the survivors of cities! (Num. 24:15–19)

We will first investigate where we are, then look for road signs, then observe the landmarks, and finally reflect on how Christ can change us through the passage. When we study a passage, it is not always necessary to look at these aspects in this exact order. Sometimes it might be helpful to go back and forth to examine and reexamine some of these aspects. But each perspective adds richness and increases the accuracy of our understanding, so we want to consider them all.

You Are Here

We first look at the circumstances of the original partici-pants in the events and audience of the biblical book. We also want to see where the passage fits in the larger lay of the land, the covenant stream that flows through biblical history from start to finish. In this case, we will postpone looking at other related passages that are farther away, and also defer for the moment analyzing the original purpose of the passage, until after we have examined the road signs and the landmarks.

This passage is part of the Pentateuch, the five books of Moses that open the Old Testament and set the scene for everything that follows. Numbers 24 describes an event that took place in the wilderness, before Israel entered the promised land. When Moses wrote about this prophecy of Balaam, God had already given Adam and Eve the promise of salvation through their descendant (Gen. 3:15). He had also made the covenant with Noah, that he would preserve living creatures on earth, and with Abraham, that he would multiply his descendants and give them a land. Moses himself had already received the law on Mount Sinai. Now Israel was about to cross over the Jordan with the purpose of establishing a nation that lives according to God's commandments. Since we know that all of Scripture is about fulfilling the plan of salvation, we know that this prophecy tells us something about the fulfillment of the covenant promises and tells us something about Jesus.

When we focus on the nearest contexts of Numbers 24, we need to keep two sets of circumstances in view. First, there is the situation of Moses and the wilderness generation, moving slowly but surely toward the promised land. The Lord had already given his people victory over Sihon, king of the Amorites, and Og, king of Bashan. As a result, the leaders of Moab and Midian, led by King Balak, were terrified by Israel's advance. They bribed Balaam to invoke a curse that would weaken or destroy the people of Israel. Balaam was a strange character. Although he was willing to take money to try to curse the Lord's people, still God gave true prophecies through this corrupt prophet. Though warned by the Lord that he must not curse this people whom God blessed, Balaam tried repeatedly to earn the reward that Balak offered by speaking words of power to harm the Israelites. Each time Balaam tried to speak evil, Israel's divine Protector "overrode" his attempts and compelled him to speak further good instead.

Second, we also need to keep in mind the circumstances of the next generations of Israelites, who received the books of Moses as they faced the daunting challenges of invading Canaan under Joshua's leadership. Moses' record of Balaam's unwilling prophecy of blessing would bolster their confidence in the Lord's power to overcome the entrenched pagan peoples who occupied the land that the Lord had promised to Abraham's descendants.

Road Signs

The references to Jacob and Israel (another name for Jacob) are road signs that point to God's previous promises to the patriarchs. Phrases such as "a star shall come out of Jacob," the "one from Jacob" who "shall exercise dominion," and the "scepter" that "shall rise out of Israel" point to a King, to the coming Messiah, who will be a descendant of Jacob (Matt. 2:2). The scepter reminds us of an earlier prophecy, when Jacob blessed his sons, the heads of the twelve tribes of Israel, before his death. He said that "the scepter shall not depart from Judah" (Gen. 49:10), the tribe from which David and Jesus himself would come. In Revelation 22:16, Jesus is called the "root and descendant of David, the bright morning star."

Another road sign is the basic prediction of Balaam's prophecy that God would destroy the Israelites' enemies and give his people the promised land. This takes us back to the promise made to Abraham, secured by God's own life in the ratification ceremony that we studied earlier in chapter 2. The fulfillment of God's promises to Abraham is a key description of the Lord's whole work of salvation throughout the Bible (Ex. 32:13; Deut. 29:13; Ps. 105:9, 42; Rom. 4:13, 16; Gal. 3:13–14).

Landmarks

King

The language of Balaam's oracle identifies a king who would arise in Israel to conquer and wield sovereignty over other nations. A *star* (Isa. 14:12; Matt. 2:2), a *scepter* (Gen. 49:10; Pss. 45:6; 60:7), and exercising *dominion* are images of royal power. The use of the scepter to "crush the forehead of Moab," the nation that would pay Balaam richly if only he would curse Israel, brings into view the military victory of the Ruler who would arise out of Israel, and reminds us of the promise of the coming offspring of Eve who would "bruise [the] head" of the serpent (Gen. 3:15).

Prophet

There is an obvious contrast between the prophet Balaam, who intended and tried to speak lies, and the final Prophet, Jesus, whose heart desires to speak only the truth. Jesus is himself "the way, and the truth, and the life" (John 14:6). But there is a similarity in the final result: Balaam did in fact speak God's truth, as does Jesus.

Other Related Passages

Now let's look at other passages related to the prophecy of Balaam, but not as close in time or situation to the wilderness and conquest generations. Perhaps the most striking thing about Balaam's language is the way in which he contrasts his own time to the time of Israel's future, triumphant Ruler: "I see him, but *not now*; I behold him, but *not near*" (Num. 24:17). In the "geography" of the Bible's redemptive history, this strange prophet-for-hire knew that his time and place were far, far away from the "metropolis," from the arrival of Israel's coming King, who would wield dominion over the nations of the world. Not surprisingly, at such a distance all that Balaam could decipher about the coming King's conquest was phrased in the terms of destruction and dispossession, without a hint of grace. Only as Israel's coming King drew near would the details of his victory, blending strict justice with lavish grace, come into sharper focus.

Two bridges span Lake Hodges, near our former home in southern California. One bridge supports a six-lane superhighway, Interstate 15, which carries over two hundred thousand vehicles daily, from motorcycles to massive semi-trucks, all traveling at high speed. The other, running parallel to the interstate two or three hundred yards to the west, is a footbridge for pedestrians. When hikers on the path around the lake reach its western shore and look back toward the east, they experience a bizarre optical illusion: the two bridges appear to be one, and walkers seem to be strolling only a few feet from trucks barreling south at seventy miles an hour! As you get closer, you can see the separation between the bridges and the traffic that each is carrying. Biblical prophecies are often like this. They are fulfilled in different stages; but from a distance, the various fulfillments look like a single event. We can tell from Balaam's words "not now" and "not near" that he somehow sensed that he stood far away from the fulfillment of the words of blessing that God had forced him to speak. He simply could not see all the details. Only the unfolding of history would enable us to recognize the different stages of fulfillment.

So when and by whom was Balaam's prophecy fulfilled? Several answers seem to fit:

David

We find a first fulfillment in King David, who defeated the Moabites, made the whole Moabite army lie down on the ground, and killed two-thirds of them (2 Sam. 8:2). David went on to conquer other surrounding nations as well: Edom (whose dispossession Balaam predicted, Num. 24:19), Amalek (whose destruction Balaam foresaw, Num. 24:20), Syria, Ammon, and Philistia (2 Sam. 8:5–14). That might be as far as Balaam could see into the future, since his whole prophecy focuses on how Israel's King will defeat, destroy, and subdue other nations.

Later Bible passages bring into view glorious and gracious details that Balaam could not see clearly from afar. Future events and prophecies show that David was not the final victorious King who was to come. For example, the prophet Amos in the eighth century B.C. foresaw the fall of Judah and the destruction of Jerusalem, which would occur in the sixth century B.C. (Amos 2:4–5). In those events the dynasty of David would be humiliated and deprived of royal power. But Amos also saw a day when God would reverse this judgment:

> "In that day I will raise up
>   the booth of David that is fallen
> and repair its breaches,
>   and raise up its ruins
>   and rebuild it as in the days of old,
> that they may possess the remnant of Edom
>   and all the nations who are called by my name,"
>   declares the Lord who does this. (Amos 9:11–12)

The restoration of David's royal "booth" is described in terms that involve military power and the dispossession of Edom from its territory southeast of the Dead Sea, as we heard in

Balaam's oracle. But Amos's mention of "nations who are called by my name" alludes to God's promise to Abraham—long before Balaam—that through Abraham's offspring the nations would be blessed. In the wider context of God's commitment to Abraham, already secured by the time Balaam came along, we have reason to expect that Israel's victorious Monarch will bring the nations not only destruction, but also blessing (Gen. 12:3).

Jesus

The prophet Zechariah predicted that the righteous King who was still to come would be humble, riding on a donkey, and that he would bring salvation:

> Rejoice greatly, O daughter of Zion!
>   Shout aloud, O daughter of Jerusalem!
> Behold, your king is coming to you;
>   righteous and having salvation is he,
> humble and mounted on a donkey,
>   on a colt, the foal of a donkey. (Zech. 9:9)

As we have seen, the Gospels identify Jesus as the true King. He said that his miracles were evidence that the kingdom of God had come (Matt. 12:28), and his preaching announced the inauguration of the kingdom of God (9:35). He entered Jerusalem triumphantly as a king (Mark 11), even on a donkey, as foretold by Zechariah. When Pilate asked Jesus if he was the king of the Jews, Jesus answered that he was, but explained that his kingdom was not the kind that Pilate was thinking of, for it was not "of this world" (John 18:33–37). Then the Sovereign God used Pilate to make sure that the sign posted over Jesus' head on the cross proclaimed him as the King (19:19–22).

The Growth of the Church

As we move into the book of Acts, the risen Jesus explains to his disciples even more about the nature of his kingdom. They ask whether he is going to restore the kingdom to Israel. Jesus gives an answer that might have been a bit confusing to them:

> He said to them, "It is not for you to know times or seasons that the Father has fixed by his own authority. But you will receive power when the Holy Spirit has come upon you, and you will be my witnesses in Jerusalem and in all Judea and Samaria, and to the end of the earth." (Acts 1:7–8)

The kingdom will be established not by human power, but by the power of the Holy Spirit. The weapon that will subdue the nations is not a sword, but the preaching of the gospel. The kingdom of God is much bigger and more powerful than the disciples were thinking, and it is eternal.

Another step forward in biblical history brings us to a fulfillment of Amos's prophecy in Acts 15. An assembly of apostles and church elders met in Jerusalem after the first missionary journey of Paul and Barnabas. As the council sought to discern how to regard Gentiles who trusted in Jesus, testimonies offered by Peter, Paul, and Barnabas showed that God had welcomed believing Gentiles without requiring that they be circumcised. James then put these testimonies into a biblical context, commenting, "Simeon [Peter] has related how God first visited the Gentiles, to take from them a people for his name" (Acts 15:14). James then demonstrated that this development fulfilled Old Testament prophecy, citing Amos's prediction of the reconstruction of David's dynasty to rule over nations (that is, Gentiles), who would bear God's name. God's recent acts confirmed, said James, that David's Great Son, Jesus, would conquer Edom and other Gentiles not by violence or armies, but by the gospel of grace applied by the invincible power of the Holy Spirit, inviting Gentiles to bear the Lord's name, rejoicing to become his willing and grateful possession.

The Second Coming of Christ

Finally, the main theme of the book of Revelation, the last book in the Bible, is the ultimate victory of Christ. Heaven is opened to show his glory, and the scrolls of history are unrolled to reveal how he will destroy all his enemies and deliver his people. Jesus is described as a great warrior riding on a white horse, his eyes like a "flame of fire," and having a sword coming out of his mouth. On his robe is written the name "King of kings and Lord of lords" (Rev. 19:11–16). Jesus will cast Satan into the lake of fire and establish the eternal kingdom with a new heaven and a new earth (Rev. 20–21). Amen! Come, Lord Jesus!

What Balaam glimpsed at a distance the apostles eventually saw "up close." The first fulfillment of the promises was David, but he was only a faint figure of the true King. The risen Messiah began to extend his reign across the world through the heart-captivating, life-transforming power of his grace. That kingdom expansion has changed the world and embraced even us, almost two millennia after God enthroned King Jesus at his right hand in heaven.

We began our journey to Jesus from Numbers 24, standing with that strangely conflicted prophet Balaam on Moab's plains. We saw that he caught a distant, indistinct glimpse of a future, conquering scepter-bearer. Then we watched in wonder as God, over many centuries, brought into ever-sharper focus the profile of that mighty Champion. Finally, at the appointed moment, Christ made his appearance in human history and in human nature, to conquer and captivate the hearts of the nations by his grace.

Purpose

This fourth oracle of Balaam previewed the Lord's greatest blessing to Israel, at the distance of many generations into the future. The purpose of these events for that wilderness generation, untrained in warfare, was to strengthen their trust in and deepen their allegiance to the Lord who sovereignly overruled Balaam's and Balak's malicious plot. For every successive generation whom God calls by grace, Balaam's unwitting, unwilling pronouncement of blessing through the coming King summons us to hope in God's promise and trust in God's Anointed, Jesus, our Ruler and Defender.

What Difference Does It Make to Us?

We are not finished with our study until we ask how we can apply the message of the passage we are studying to our lives and our world today. One thing we see immediately in the *events* of the story of Balaam is that the grace of God overcomes evil. God overcame evil to make his message clear, speaking even through a prophet who meant to say something else! We hear the same message in the *words* of the prophecy itself, the promise that the great King will defeat our enemies. The gospel is all about overcoming evil. Jesus has conquered evil by living his perfect life and making a perfect sacrifice for our sins. So whether it is a problem that we are currently facing, unknown struggles in our future, or even the worldwide battle with evil, we know that the ultimate victory is ours in Christ our conquering King.

Review Questions

1. List the ways that journeying with Jesus through his Word changes us.
2. Why does discovering the Bible's pervasive witness to Christ move us to worship?
3. How does the Bible move us to hope and trust by leading us to Jesus?
4. How does a focus on seeing Christ as we read the Bible make us more like him in love and holiness?
5. Explain how the author sees different fulfillments of the prophecy of Balaam in Numbers 24:15–19.

Questions for Reflection

1. As you reflect on your prior experience of reading the Bible, what has made the difference between the times when your "heart burned within you" and other times when the words of Scripture, though you knew them to be true, did not move you to marvel and worship?
2. The Gospels show how the living Lord Jesus came in person and taught his disciples how the Old Testament had foretold his sufferings and glory. Can we still expect Jesus to "come" to us today to open our minds to the Scriptures, and to open them to our understanding? How does he do this now?
3. According to Ephesians 1:3–14, what is the focal point of God's overarching purpose for history? How should God's purpose for history influence how we read the Bible, in which he has revealed his plan?
4. Think over major figures in Old Testament history—Adam and Eve, Noah, Abraham, Jacob, Moses,

David—one by one, asking this question about each one: How does this individual's story exemplify the ways in which hope in God's promise transforms lives?

5. Think over the same figures in Old Testament history, asking this question about each one: How does this individual's life story demonstrate that the person fell short, and cannot bear the weight of our hopes for redemption?

6. Think over the same figures in Old Testament history, asking this question about each one: How does Jesus exceed and excel this "hero" who preceded him (as well as each one who came after him)? How does Christ's flawless faithfulness as Lord and Servant of the covenant place our hopes for rescue and re-creation on a firm, eternal foundation?

7. When Paul affirms in 2 Corinthians 3:18 that believers, by beholding the glory of the Lord, "are being transformed into the same image," he is not implying that our physical eyes take in the visible light of God's radiance, as Moses' eyes did on Mount Sinai. So how *do* Christians today behold the Lord's glory?

8. In 2 Corinthians 3:18, Paul is not implying that our physical appearance will literally glow as Moses' face did when he descended from Mount Sinai. So how are Christians today transformed into the image of Christ?

9. Which way of reading the Bible is more practical and powerful in changing our character and behavior: To focus our attention on the Scriptures' commands and prohibitions, and on human characters as moral examples? Or to focus on how the Bible reveals Christ and his redemptive mission? Why?

10. What insight or reading strategy that you encountered in *Journeys with Jesus* is going to change how you read the Bible? Where do you plan to start?

Exercise

Select a passage of the Old Testament and go through the steps of interpretation, using the guidelines of this book to: (1) discover where you are (investigate the language, the circumstances, other related passages, and the purpose); (2) look for road signs (types of Christ); (3) look for landmarks (references to the offices of prophet, priest, and king); and (4) discover how God intends us to respond to the passage's message today. (Does it move us to marvel and worship, to hope and trust, to become more like Christ?)

You can use tools such as commentaries, dictionaries, a concordance, Bible software (for example, eSword, Logos, or BibleWorks), and reference notes or introductory comments in a study Bible.

FOR FURTHER READING

More Accessible

Barrett, Michael P. V. *Love Divine and Unfailing: The Gospel According to Hosea*. GAOT.[1] Phillipsburg, NJ: P&R Publishing, 2008.

Bergsma, Derke P. *Redemption: The Triumph of God's Great Plan*. Lansing, IL: Redeemer Books, 1989.

Boda, Mark J. *After God's Own Heart: The Gospel According to David*. GAOT. Phillipsburg, NJ: P&R Publishing, 2007.

Clowney, Edmund P. *The Unfolding Mystery: Discovering Christ in the Old Testament*. 2nd ed. Phillipsburg, NJ: P&R Publishing, 2013.

Dillard, Raymond B. *Faith in the Face of Apostasy: The Gospel According to Elijah and Elisha*. GAOT. Phillipsburg, NJ: P&R Publishing, 1999.

Drew, Charles D. *Ancient Love Song: Finding Christ in the Old Testament*. Phillipsburg, NJ: P&R Publishing, 2000.

Duguid, Iain M. *Living in the Gap between Promise and Reality: The Gospel According to Abraham*. GAOT. Phillipsburg, NJ: P&R Publishing, 1999.

———. *Living in the Grip of Relentless Grace: The Gospel According to Isaac and Jacob*. GAOT. Phillipsburg, NJ: P&R Publishing, 2002.

---

1. *GAOT* is an acronym for Gospel According to the Old Testament, a series published by P&R Publishing.

Duguid, Iain M., and Matthew P. Harmon. *Living in the Light of Inextinguishable Hope: The Gospel According to Joseph.* GAOT. Phillipsburg, NJ: P&R Publishing, 2013.

Estelle, Bryan D. *Salvation through Judgment and Mercy: The Gospel According to Jonah.* GAOT. Phillipsburg, NJ: P&R Publishing, 2005.

Eswine, Zachary W. *Recovering Eden: The Gospel According to Ecclesiastes.* GAOT. Phillipsburg, NJ: P&R Publishing, 2014.

Ferguson, Sinclair. *Preaching Christ from the Old Testament.* London: Proclamation Trust, 2002. Available at http://www.simeontrust.org/media/doc-sferguson-peachingchrist.pdf [*sic*: "peaching"].

Goldsworthy, Graeme. *According to Plan: The Unfolding Revelation of God in the Bible.* Downers Grove, IL: IVP Academic, 2002.

Gregory, Bryan. *Longing for God in an Age of Discouragement: The Gospel According to Zechariah.* GAOT. Phillipsburg, NJ: P&R Publishing, 2010.

Jackson, David R. *Crying Out for Vindication: The Gospel According to Job.* GAOT. Phillipsburg, NJ: P&R Publishing, 2007.

Longman, Tremper, III. *Immanuel in Our Place: Seeing Christ in Israel's Worship.* GAOT. Phillipsburg, NJ: P&R Publishing, 2001.

Murray, David. *Jesus on Every Page: Ten Simple Ways to Seek and Find Christ in the Old Testament.* Nashville, TN: Thomas Nelson, 2013.

Schwab, George M. *Hope in the Midst of a Hostile World: The Gospel According to Daniel.* GAOT. Phillipsburg, NJ: P&R Publishing, 2006.

———. *Right in Their Own Eyes: The Gospel According to Judges.* GAOT. Phillipsburg, NJ: P&R Publishing, 2011.

Selvaggio, Anthony T. *From Bondage to Liberty: The Gospel According to Moses.* GAOT. Phillipsburg, NJ: P&R Publishing, 2014.

Ulrich, Dean R. *From Famine to Fullness: The Gospel According to Ruth.* GAOT. Phillipsburg, NJ: P&R Publishing, 2007.

Wright, Christopher J. H. *Knowing Jesus through the Old Testament.* Downers Grove, IL: IVP Academic, 1995.

More Advanced

Beale, G. K. *Handbook on the New Testament Use of the Old Testament: Exegesis and Interpretation*. Grand Rapids: Baker Academic, 2012.

Goldsworthy, Graeme. *Gospel-Centered Hermeneutics: Foundations and Principles of Evangelical Biblical Interpretation*. Downers Grove, IL: InterVarsity Press, 2010.

———. *Preaching the Whole Bible as Christian Scripture: The Application of Biblical Theology to Expository Preaching*. Grand Rapids: Eerdmans, 2000.

Horton, Michael. *Introducing Covenant Theology*. Grand Rapids: Baker, 2009.

Johnson, Dennis E. *Him We Proclaim: Preaching Christ from All the Scriptures*. Phillipsburg, NJ: P&R Publishing, 2007.

Robertson, O. Palmer. *The Christ of the Covenants*. Phillipsburg, NJ: P&R Publishing, 1981.

———. *The Christ of the Prophets*. Phillipsburg, NJ: P&R Publishing, 2008.

———. *The Christ of Wisdom: A Redemptive-Historical Exploration of the Wisdom Books of the Old Testament*. Phillipsburg, NJ: P&R Publishing, 2017.

INDEX OF SCRIPTURE

7:1–3—107
7:1–28—107
7:3—107
7:11–28—106
7:14—107
7:26–27—113
8:1—107
8:1–5—112
8:1–6—107
8:4–6—107
8:5—80
8:6—30
8:13—27
9:1–28—107
9:9–10—89
9:11–12—107
9:11–14—112
9:13—89
9:13–14—114
9:14—89
9:15—30
9:26–28—112
10:1–22—107
10:5–10—33

10:8—67
10:9–14—67
10:11–12—107
10:12–18—114
10:19–22—112
11:8–12—84
11:17–19—84
12:2—107
12:18–29—106
12:24—30
12:28–29—107
13:5—127
13:7–8—106
13:8—127
13:10–16—107
13:15–16—86, 114
13:22—106

James
2:21—66
2:24—66

1 Peter
1:8—135

1:10–11—100
1:11—11, 18
1:18–19—114
1:19—90
2:4–5—86, 112
2:5—114
2:7—2
2:24—114
3:20—84
4:10—12

2 Peter
1:16–18—135
2:5—84

Revelation
1:10–20—110
4:1–6—110
7:14—114
12:11—115
19:11–16—115, 148
21:2—112
21:9–26—112
22:16—142

INDEX OF SUBJECTS AND NAMES

ALSO BY DENNIS E. JOHNSON

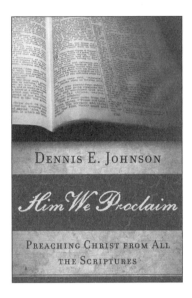

Challenging modern preachers to expound the Bible like Peter and Paul, *Him We Proclaim* makes the hermeneutical and historical case for a return to apostolic preaching—preaching that is Christ-centered, redemptive-historical, missiologically communicated, and grounded in grace. But moving beyond theory, *Him We Proclaim* provides examples of how this method applies to all Old and New Testament genres—history, law, psalm, prophecy, and doctrine and exhortation.

"This book holds the promise of the recovery of biblical preaching for those who will give themselves to the demanding and glorious task of setting each text within the context of God's redemptive plan. This is a book that belongs on every preacher's bookshelf."

—R. Albert Mohler Jr.

Dennis E. Johnson (ThM, Westminster Theological Seminary; PhD, Fuller Theological Seminary) taught New Testament and practical theology at Westminster Seminary California for more than thirty-five years. He is an ordained minister in the Presbyterian Church in America, the author of *Him We Proclaim* and of commentaries on Acts, Philippians, Hebrews, and Revelation (*Triumph of the Lamb*), and a contributor to several study Bibles and other books. He and his wife, Jane, live in Dayton, Tennessee.